Energy Healing *for* Modern Life

About the Author

Jessica Howard brings twenty years of energy healing expertise to her work as an author, teacher, and practitioner. A reiki master who has studied numerous healing traditions, she's spoken at international conferences and contributed to spiritual publications, including *Watkins* magazine. Her approach blends traditional wisdom with modern applications, and she offers workshops and healing sessions in London.

Energy Healing *for* Modern Life

Embrace Your Energetic Self and Find Your Well-Being

JESSICA HOWARD

WOODBURY, MINNESOTA

First Edition
First Printing, 2026

Cover design by Kevin R. Brown
Editing by Stephanie Finne
Interior art by Llewellyn Art Department

Library of Congress Cataloging-in-Publication Data (Pending)
ISBN: 978-0-7387-8235-5

Llewellyn Publications
A Division of Llewellyn Worldwide Ltd.
2143 Wooddale Drive
Woodbury, MN 55125-2989
www.llewellyn.com

Printed in the United States of America

GPSR Representation:
UPI-2M PLUS d.o.o., Medulićeva 20, 10000 Zagreb, Croatia
matt.parsons@upi2mbooks.hr

Contents

Exercise List *ix*

Disclaimer *xi*

Introduction *1*

Chapter One: The Foundations of Energy Work 5

Chapter Two: Connecting with Energy 25

Chapter Three: Hygiene and Best Practise 45

Chapter Four: Energy Healing 59

Chapter Five: Building a Cohesive Practice 173

Chapter Six: Energy and Your Environment 181

Closing Words *207*

Recommended Reading *209*

Bibliography *211*

Index *213*

Exercises

Chapter Two

Beginner's Meditation Exercise 28

Grounding—Roots Meditation 30

Centring—Roots Extended 31

The Calming Seas Centring Method 33

The Vase Breath 35

The Three-Part Breath 36

Nine Breaths of Purification 36

The Lion's Breath 37

Creating an Energy Orb 38

Crystal Energy Exercise 41

Chapter Three

Building Your Energy Shield 47

Programming Your Shield to Absorb Negative Energy 48

Shielding Against Deliberate Energy Attacks 49

The Double-Layered Shield 49

Performing an Egg Cleanse 56

Chapter Four

Performing a Body Scan 63

Colour Association Exercise 66

Knocking on the Door of Life (Also Known as the Spinning Drum) 74

Pulling Down the Heavens 76

Pushing the Wave 77

How to Perform an EFT Tapping Healing 83

Performing a Chakra Energy Scan 100

Meditation One: Quick Chakra Empowerment 101

Meditation Two: Chakra Cleanse Meditation 102

How to See Auras 108

Aura Programming Exercise 111

Performing a Reiki Healing Session 115

Connecting with Angelic Energies for Healing 119

Creating Healing Water 155

How to Make a Poppet 168

Chapter Six

Performing a Smoke Cleanse 196

Creating Your Own Healing Sanctuary 204

Disclaimer

The publisher and author assume no liability for any injuries caused to the reader that may result from the reader's use of content contained in this publication. The information in this book is not intended to diagnose or treat any medical or emotional condition and must not be used as a replacement for proper medical care. Consulting with a trusted physical and mental healthcare practitioner is always recommended before beginning any exercise regimen or change in diet, and common sense is strongly urged when contemplating employment of the practices and substances described in this work.

Introduction

Welcome to this book on energy work and energy healing. I firmly believe that working with energy is one of the fundamental spiritual practices; everything in this world, in this universe, is made from and connected by energy. By working with and becoming in tune with this energy, we can find peace, strength, and empowerment. We can take control of our lives, understand our hopes and dreams, and grow into our full potential. I know it sounds like I'm promising a lot, and I know that there are many books, websites, and people out there who will tell you that you can be the best version of yourself if you just follow their teachings. So, what makes this any different?

My own journey into energy work started more than twenty years ago when I first encountered the chakras. From that moment on, I was hooked, and understanding more about this energy and how it can enrich our lives became a lifelong passion. This book is a culmination of all I have learned and experienced, but even now after all this time I am still finding more to learn and new ways to practise. One of my previous roles was as an elder in a community, where I began teaching lessons on energy work. I loved being able to guide others in their journey, and so this book felt like the natural next step for me; I am very excited that this is a journey you too have decided to undertake!

We embody spiritual energy, and it is forever present in the world around us. We interact with this energy constantly on a day-to-day basis. As such, working with energy isn't something that only requires an elaborate ritual once a month that you can then forget about until the next month, but rather, regular practice. Incorporating elements such as cleansing, protection, and healing into your day-to-day life is necessary to embrace the full potential of your energetic being. As cliche as it may sound, it really is a way of life; as you might visit the gym a couple of times a week or make sure to drink several glasses of water a day to keep your physical health in check, everything in this book can be utilised regularly to keep your energetic self healthy.

How to Use This Book

This book is designed to be an introduction to energy work with a specific focus on energy healing. Energy work is a vast subject, having been around for thousands of years and present through a variety of different cultures and traditions. There are various methods, techniques, and teachings to learn from. This book encompasses not just energy healing itself but also everything you will need to know to get you to the point where you are ready to heal, and beyond. We will begin with understanding what energy is, the dangers and ethical considerations of energy work, cleansing and protection, and sensing this universal energy both within you and around you, and that's before we even get to energy healing itself! However, even with so much to get through, I am conscious that there is a lot I'm leaving out.

I have deliberately focused on the practical application of the various techniques and methods we will cover, wanting to give you real experience through meditations and exercises rather than focus too much on the theory. Many of the subjects I cover in this book—such as protection, chakras, auras, and crystal healing for example—can (and have) fill entire books alone! With so much information out there, I wanted to focus on giving you just enough information to be able to get started but also give you space to do your own research on any areas that particularly interest you. So, think of this book as one more tool in your arsenal, a reference to guide you in your own journey with energy.

One of the main lessons you should take from this book is that everyone interacts with energy differently, and so you may find that you are stronger with some exercises than others. Or there may be certain methods or exercises within this book that just don't fit in with your own personal belief system—I know people who work with auras but don't subscribe to chakras for example. Whilst these may seem intrinsic to one another, there is plenty of scope to define your own way of interacting with, and working with, energy. As such, I've tried to avoid a "this is the only right way" approach with this book and instead have endeavoured to present the information in a way that gives you the freedom to experience, learn, and create your own system.

Chapter Breakdown

We will start with the very basics in chapter 1—what energy is, why practise it, the ethics of energy work, and the dangers associated with it. In chapter 2, we begin our hands-on work with energy with some simple, practical exercises to help you attune to energy. This chapter will be crucial as we move through this book, as you need to be able to connect with energy before you can use it for healing.

In chapter 3, we will look at energetic hygiene and best practice, with a specific focus on grounding, centring, finding your own power centre, cleansing, and protection. I appreciate that you may be excited to move on to energy healing itself, but by ensuring that you have mastered the exercises in chapter 3 will build a strong foundation from which you can then start to heal from.

Chapter 4 is the chapter you've most likely been waiting for, and it is dedicated to various methods of energy healing, such as using colour, chakras, auras, EFT tapping, and more. It is by far the biggest section of the book! Along with the different applications of energy healing, we will also take a closer look at how to perform energy healing on other people, as well as useful tools that you can incorporate into your healings.

In chapter 5, we will take everything that we have learned in the previous chapters and look at building our own cohesive, sustainable practice. Energy healing shouldn't be a "one and done" activity, but you will be surprised at the number of people who fall into the trap of thinking so. When we incorporate these practices into our everyday lives, we truly start to realise the benefits that connecting with our energetic selves has, as well as the peace and happiness it can provide.

Finally, in chapter 6, we will look at energy and our environment. This includes both our home and our external environments. I wanted to include this section because, as you will see as we journey through this book, ensuring that we are surrounding ourselves with positive energy and protecting ourselves against negative energy is important if you wish for your energy healing to be successful long-term. If you are surrounding yourself with negative, or unbalanced, energies, then you will find that any benefits you gain from an energy healing session will be short-lived. Similarly, you will find it more difficult to actually perform energy healing in the first place when you are subjected to such energies. As such, ensuring that your environment is also an energetically healthy one is an aspect that should not be overlooked.

Remember to take everything within these pages at your own pace and make sure that you feel comfortable before progressing. This is your journey; not mine, not your partner's, or anyone else's. It isn't a race or a tick box exercise you can run through in a day and then proclaim yourself a "master." It is a spiritual journey, a chance for you to transform and grow, and the only measures of success are the ones you define for yourself.

What You'll Need

Before we get started, I recommend that you find a journal to record your experiences. I know every book on every similar subject will recommend you work with a journal, so this won't be anything revolutionary to you. But considering that everyone experiences energy differently, recording exactly how you feel and the thoughts and impressions that come to you through the various exercises will really help you understand how you personally experience energy. As we work our way through this book, I will be providing journal prompts and/or exercises at the end of each chapter to give you a chance to utilise what we have learned throughout, so make sure it is one that provides you with plenty of space to write about your experiences.

So, without further ado, let's get started!

CHAPTER ONE
The Foundations of Energy Work

This chapter is dedicated to the "need to know" information. While I know you may be excited to jump straight in and try your hand at some energy work, please make sure you read this chapter thoroughly first. Understanding exactly what energy is and what we mean when we use the term *negative energy* is fundamental to being able to practise it successfully.

As well as attempting to define what energy is (which is not as easy as it sounds) and specifically what negative energy is, we will also briefly look at why energy healing is so important. We will then consider the ethical conundrums we may face when working with energy, as well as the dangers. It is normal when embarking on a new practice or a new subject to feel a sense of uncertainty or a fear of the unknown, and whilst I don't discuss elements such as dangers to scare you, it is important to be informed. The good news is that everything you learn in this book will adequately aid you in avoiding those dangers, so make sure you don't skip any of the sections, no matter how simplistic or boring it may seem. Oftentimes the simplest approaches can be the most effective.

What Is Energy?

So, what exactly is energy? This is a difficult question to answer, and there is no one agreed upon definition. Working with energy has been a part of many different cultures and civilisations for hundreds of years, and each one has a different name for energy and a different way for understanding and connecting with it. In Sanskrit it is known as *prana*, and we can use the chakras and forms of moving meditation, such as yoga, to help us work with this energy. In traditional Chinese culture and Chinese medicine, it is called *Qi* (sometimes written as "Chi"), which is funnelled through energy channels in the body known as meridians.

Physical practices such as Tai Chi and Qi Gong can help us connect with this energy, whilst healing practices such as reflexology and acupuncture utilise these meridians to bring us the relief we need. In the West, it is often referred to as energy, divine energy, or universal energy. I personally use the term *universal energy*, and I will be continuing with that as we make our way through this book.

The one thing that the majority of these beliefs have in common is the agreement that everything is made of energy, and this energy is within us and around us. Quantum physics has taught us that yes, everything is made of energy, but we are talking about a different sort of energy—a spiritual energy. There have been plenty of studies done in a more scientific capacity to try and prove the existence of this spiritual energy and its impact on the human body. If this is an area that interests you, then I recommend looking up the International Society for the Study of Subtle Energies and Energy Medicine.[1] This nonprofit was established in the 1980s, and for a time they released a quarterly journal called *Subtle Energies & Energy Medicine*, which contains many studies done to help explore and better understand energy and energy healing.[2] These have all been archived online and can be accessed for free, so if you are looking for studies, research papers, and the like, then this is a great place to start.

Much of what I will discuss in this book has ties to ancient mysticism and has been around for hundreds of years through these different cultures. However, there has been a modern-day resurgence around energy work. You can walk into most shops that have a magazine section and pick up some sort of lifestyle magazine that will promise to help you "manifest the best you," or articles that talk about not allowing toxic exes to ruin your "vibe."

1. "What is ISSSEEM," Holos University, accessed March 31, 2025, https://holosuniversity.org/what-is-issseem/.

2. Simon Fraser University Public Knowledge Project Archives, accessed March 31, 2025, https://journals.sfu.ca/seemj/index.php/seemj/issue/archive.

As someone who is old enough to have grown up without the internet, I think it is great! I've seen older practitioners turn their noses up and get huffy about it; they say it's all blind commercialism, people aren't learning the "right" way, and so forth. And yes, access to information has never been easier, and this does also mean access to bad information is also unfortunately all too easy if you don't know where to look. But this is an issue we are seeing in all industries and is a much larger conversation. As long as people do their research and appreciate respectfully rather than appropriate, then I personally think it is great that the need to embrace our energetic selves, as well as our physical, mental, and emotional selves, is becoming more mainstream. Don't let the naysayers keep you from practising in ways that suit your personal lifestyle and beliefs.

Energy healing—which had mostly been confined to the East—began to rise in popularity in the 1900s in the United States. However, these practices were not subject to FDA approval, or any other governing body, meaning that it was all too easy for unsafe practices to emerge and for people to find themselves at the mercy of scam artists and snake oil salesmen. As such, Congress introduced the National Center for Complementary and Alternative Medicine (NCCAM) as a part of the National Institutes of Health (NIH).

The NCCAM created a report that aimed to draw a line between scientifically verified energy and the spiritual energy we refer to when using terms such as *prana* and *universal energy*.[3] This aimed to ensure that the public is made aware as to which of the two forms of energy is being used in any healing they take part in.

First, we have veritable energy, which includes magnetism, sound, and electronic forces, using wavelengths and frequencies as a part of their healing method. (I will discuss sound healing later on in this book.) This is the type of energy that is more closely aligned with known scientific principles.

3. Erminia Guarneri and Rauni Prittinen King, "Challenges and Opportunities Faced by Biofield Practitioners in Global Health and Medicine: A White Paper," Supplement, *Global Advances in Health and Medicine* 4, no. SI (2015), 89–96, https://pmc.ncbi.nlm.nih.gov/articles/PMC4654785/.

Putative energy is the energy field that we tap into to perform reiki, reflexology, Qi Gong, and other forms of energy manipulation and healing. This putative energy is a part of us and is connected to, impacted by, and can be influenced by our physical, mental, and emotional selves. In the same way we look after these other aspects of ourselves, we should also look after our energetic selves, and it is this concept that forms the basis of this book. We should learn to cleanse and protect our energy, to heal it and nurture it, and to work with it to help us in manifesting what it is we need from life.

In short, energy is difficult to define, although many have attempted to do so. My personal view is that Qi, prana, and the other various names used describe the same thing: universal energy. This is because this energy is present in everything and everyone—from the tiniest grains of sand to the stars that glisten in the farthest reaches of space—this energy connects us all. It cannot be created and cannot be destroyed. It is not positive, it isn't negative, it simply is, and it is our actions and our intentions that influence it to be either one. It is the unseen power that guides Earth around the sun, that draws the tides to the moon, and that allows the first flowers to bloom as spring is ushered in. This energy is life itself, the very essence of existence. By learning how to interact with it, to heal it, and to cherish it, we can find our place in the world and experience everything the world has to offer with love, hope, and joy in our hearts.

What Is Negative Energy?

I imagine that *negative energy* is a term that you are already quite familiar with; it is one that has definitely become more present in the mainstream in recent years. In the next chapter of this book particularly, we will be using the term *negative energy* a lot. So, what exactly is negative energy?

Energy itself is neutral. It isn't good, bad, positive, or negative. It is our intention and the intention of others that can turn energy into positive or negative. So negative energy is that which has been tainted in some way, usually by negative emotion, negative thoughts, or negative actions.

In my experience, negative energy will most often build up over time. It is not very often that I have walked into a place or met a person and experienced an immediate sense of negative energy being present (although it does happen). Often it starts small, so small that you may barely notice.

Let's say, for example, that you slept through your alarm and didn't have time to shower before you left the house. Not a big deal, but you definitely don't feel as fresh as you would like. You get on the train and there are no seats—again, not a big deal, but your back is aching slightly, and it would have been nice to get a seat. You get to the office and the lift is broken, so you have to take the stairs—considering you've just had to stand on the train, this feels like a bit more of an inconvenience. Throughout the day these little things continue. As isolated incidents, they are perfectly manageable. However, we can become more and more annoyed as they begin to build on top of each other, and whether we consciously realise it or not, we can begin to harbour this negativity within ourselves.

We might just be having a bad day; it is a one-off occurrence, then we have a good sleep and wake up the next day having completely forgotten about the frustrations of the day before. But sometimes this energy can sit with us for a more prolonged period. Maybe a long-term illness or a toxic environment that you are regularly exposed to is creating this negativity, a negativity that perhaps you are so used to now that you don't even register it. Or maybe your subconscious is deliberately burying it because it is easier than facing it. Unfortunately, whether you consciously notice it or not, your body will, and it will hold on to this negative energy. Other people may start to pick up on it also, especially those who are empathetic or able to sense energy easily.

In these sorts of situations, cleansing and protective work is very beneficial, but it will never cure the root of the problem. You will always be at risk of these negative energies sneaking their way back in. It is best, where possible, to completely remove yourself from these situations and people. To give you an idea as to how long these energies can linger, some months ago I visited the Old Operating Theatre in London. This space originally served as a garret, a place where herbs were dried for the apothecary for

St Thomas' Hospital in the Victorian age. In 1822, they added an operating theatre to the site, a theatre where they specifically operated on women. It was closed in 1862 and moved to a different part of London to make way for the London Bridge station and associated developments, and it was essentially forgotten until its rediscovery in 1956. It was then opened as a museum in 1962.[4]

The first part of the museum, the garret, was a pretty pleasant experience—full of dried herbs with descriptions of how they would have been used—with a scavenger hunt for children to follow around the museum. At the end of the garret, you pass through a short corridor and into the operating theatre itself, which is a small, windowless room. The original medical "bed" sits in the middle of what looks like an auditorium, with several raised benches at the back so trainee doctors and the like could observe operations taking place.

It wasn't an immediate reaction, but it wasn't long before I began to sense this negative energy that was foreboding, fearful, and nervous. It felt like a hand gripping around my heart and squeezing tightly. The pain and the suffering that women over the years must have endured in the operating theatre (as they often didn't use anaesthetic) was still present beneath the fresh coats of paint and polished floor. I ended up having to leave quite quickly, but to me this really emphasises this point; even now, more than 160 years later, considering all of the work that has been done to it and all of the people who come to learn and view the museum, the negative energies associated with the brutal operations they performed on women still lingered after all that time.

What does negative energy feel like? Again, this will all depend on you and how you personally connect with energy. There are times that it can manifest in physical symptoms, such as your hairs standing up on end, a tingling sensation in the skin, or headaches. I must stress that if you are experiencing any unusual physical symptoms, first and foremost see a medical doctor. It is always important to rule out the mundane before turning

4. "About Us," The Old Operating Theatre Museum and Herb Garret, accessed March 31, 2025, https://oldoperatingtheatre.com/about-us/.

to the mystical. Always visit your general practitioner if you are experiencing unexplained or prolonged physical symptoms.

You may also experience mental symptoms, such as a sudden and unexplainable feeling of fear or anxiety or unwanted mental images. Again, these can also be signs of stress, depression, and other ailments a doctor can help you with, so please reach out to a general practitioner as your first port of call if these are persistent or prolonged.

Finally, if you wear any sort of protective amulets or have any protective charms set up, these breaking can be a sign that there is negative energy surrounding you. This is usually caused by the object having absorbed all of that negative energy, so if this happens then cleanse yourself and your space and bolster your protection.

When you become more adept at energy work, you will be able to sense different types of negative energy. The energy feels very different from someone who is feeling blue because they have had a frustrating day or someone who is intentionally harbouring harmful thoughts or a desire to harm others. If you have been exposed to negative energy, then you should seek to identify the source and remove it (or remove yourself, such as from a room or a situation) before cleansing yourself/your space, and then practising some form of protection. Exactly how you do this will be revealed in chapter 2 of this book.

Why Practice Energy Healing?

As we have established, this energy is an intrinsic part of our being. It is very difficult to completely remove ourselves from situations that may expose us to negative energy. This negative energy can have a detrimental impact on ourselves, especially if we allow it to build up over time. Many practitioners engage in some sort of energy healing to help cleanse and heal themselves of this negative energy.

It is easy to think of our spiritual self as something separate from our physical, mental, and emotional selves, but this couldn't be further from the truth. With our energy being so intertwined with our other states of being, poor physical health or an emotionally traumatic experience can have a negative effect on our energy. Similarly, if we are focusing purely on our spiritual selves but not looking after the rest of ourselves, we will never truly be able to heal our energy. No matter how much you put into your spiritual self it won't be enough to overcome any deep-rooted negativity stored in your other selves.

If you want to give yourself the best shot at succeeding at energy work, then you need to look after yourself as a whole—physically, mentally, and emotionally. This may seem obvious, but it is surprisingly easy to stop taking care of yourself, especially when you are busy or stressed with life. Often this may mean changing certain aspects of our lifestyles or ridding ourselves of unhealthy behaviours we may be using as coping mechanisms. This can often feel overwhelming, as it can be difficult to build new habits and routines. My advice is to start small; even just five minutes of exercise or drinking one glass of water a day over a prolonged period will give you the foundations you need to form these life-long habits. I am in no way qualified to give medical or mental health advice, so I will avoid doing it here, but there are plenty of resources out there to help you best manage your physical, mental, and emotional health.

It is important to strengthen and protect ourselves and our own energy, but we also need to be aware of the effect that those around us can have on our energy, and vice versa. Have you ever spent time with someone who is just generally a bit miserable, and it has made you feel down too? Or someone is acting a bit erratically and it has made you feel nervous and on edge? This is an energetic reaction to their energy. When we are feeling out of sorts, we can subconsciously affect others with the energy we are putting out into the world.

It is widely believed that our energy is not just kept within our physical selves but also stretches out and forms layers of energy around us. Think about your day-to-day life; how many people do you interact with closely? For some of us, this may include standing on cramped trains or having to navigate the crowds in busy supermarkets. In each of these instances, our energy will be mingling with the energy of others, which leaves us vulnerable to the effects this can have. It is important to make sure that you know how to protect and heal your own energy, which is why a large portion of this book will be dedicated to the different methods you could use to help you heal not just your energy, but the energy of others too.

Your First Lesson

There is one very important lesson that I have learned that I want to pass on to you now, here at the very beginning of this book. Out of everything I have learned in my more than twenty years of practice, this teaching is by far the one that has made the most difference to my spiritual growth. This is the notion that like attracts like, and this applies to energy work and healing also.

If we fill our lives with positivity and strive to send positivity into the world, we are more likely to attract it. Similarly, if we constantly surround ourselves with negativity, even with the best will in the world, we will never find peace within ourselves. This may sound simple, but it can be surprisingly difficult.

To give you an example, I live in a city that is renowned for its tourism. It can be extremely frustrating just trying to get from A to B and having to dodge large crowds of people just standing around, taking photos, with little thought for those of us who actually have somewhere to be. I used to end up getting to my destination feeling stressed and angry, which is never a good mindset to start your working day or an evening out with your friends. So, I reframed the way that I thought; instead of feeling angry that these people were getting in my way and focusing on the negatives, I focus instead on the positives. I see them as friends and family, sharing their love with one another and making memories that will last a lifetime. I wonder how long they had to save up to afford this trip, how difficult it was for them to get the time off to fly all this way, how maybe these trips are one of the only points throughout the year they all get to be with each other. Over time, I have come to find myself filled with a genuine sense of love, compassion, and happiness for these people, instead of frustration and anger.

Reframing your way of thinking and focusing on finding and celebrating these positives can have a huge impact on our energetic selves and our general well-being. There are plenty of ways we can do this, including daily mantras (a phrase we repeat to ourselves), writing in a gratitude journal (I personally have an app on my phone where I write what I am grateful for every day), or actively trying to do one act of kindness per day, for example. However you approach fostering this mindset, if there is one lesson you take away that will make a difference in your life, I really hope it is this.

The Ethics of Energy Work

There are some ethical concerns around energy work that it is useful to consider before we start the doing. As with most ethical conundrums, there are no wrong or right answers. I have the answers that *I* would give to each of the questions below, but everyone's moral compass swings differently and you may disagree with my views here. However, it is not my intention to tell you what is ethically wrong or right, but to provide you with my own point of view so that you may begin to answer these questions for yourself. This will help you start to forge your own path and your own boundaries. Being able to establish and maintain boundaries is important in energy work, and in general, it is a skill that can help us in many different parts of our lives.

Consent

Consent is the expressed permission, usually from another person, for something to change or happen. Do you think it is acceptable to send healing energy to someone without their consent? Do you believe you should even need to ask for consent if you are working for their benefit and with nothing but positive intention?

It used to be my belief that no, you did not need consent, but I have learned through experience that it is a bit more complicated than that. Energy healing can be very direct, and I have noticed that for those who aren't expecting it, this sudden influx of energy can be a very uncomfortable experience. This definitely made me rethink my stance on consent. Now I only send it to those who have requested it, or I ask the universe to send this energy to the recipient only if they are open to receiving it, and to otherwise please send this healing energy to where it is most needed.

Karmic Consequence

Do you believe there are any karmic consequences attached to energy work? For example, if you decide to direct negative energy at someone, or them to you, do you believe the sender will also experience negative energy as though there were some sort of cosmic balance? What if someone is unintentionally sending negativity your way, unaware as to what it is they are doing; are there karmic consequences for this sort of negative energy attack, and would they be any different from an intentional attack?

As someone who grew up learning about witchcraft, I became acquainted very early on with the rule of three, which stipulates that what you send out will return to you multiplied by three. Whilst I don't agree with this notion exactly, I agree with the sentiment. I believe that like attracts like, and if you put negativity out into the world, you are more likely to attract negativity to you. As intention really does matter in energy work, it is my personal belief that those who are deliberately engaging with negative thoughts and behaviours will attract more negativity than someone who acts unintentionally out of frustration.

On the flipside, what if you send someone positive, healing energies—will you acquire any sort of karmic reward? Again, I believe by sending out positivity, you will receive positivity. I have also found through my own energy healing that once you really connect with and understand this energy, you find a new appreciation for the simpler things. For example, if I'm walking through town and I happen to come across pedestrian crossings all set to "go" when I need to cross the road, I'll often thank the universe for this convenience.

Do you think that sending healing energy to another could potentially take this energy away from someone who may need it more, and if so, again what could be the consequences of this? I used to use the example of going for a new job; out of several candidates, only one person can get that job, and obviously I would like it to be me. But what if there is someone worse off also applying for the job, somebody who needs the money more than me—how would I feel about taking it away from them? I would feel pretty bad, but luckily energy doesn't work like that. Whilst energy can't be created or destroyed, it can be manipulated, and this is what we do when we are healing; we manipulate the energy and set it with the intention of healing. There is plenty of energy in the universe to go around, and me using it to heal one specific person isn't going to have a large enough effect that those who maybe need it more would be denied it.

Borrowing Energy

Do you think it is okay to "take" energy from crystals, plants, and such to use to help heal? Do you believe it is okay to take other people's energy? This is a phenomenon known as *energy vampirism*, and whilst some people can accidentally drain your energy, there are some out there who do it deliberately (there are even how-to books written on the subject).

I often use crystals and plants and such in energy healing (see chapter 4). I always ask permission before borrowing any energy to use in healing by saying something along the lines of "If it is your will, please allow me to use your energy in my healing." I find that generally crystals and such are happy to give it. Even when we perform a practice such as reiki, we often ask for reiki energy to flow through us. If permission isn't granted, then often you will find that it is just impossible to connect with and use that energy. I will never use the energy of another person, even if they have given permission, because you can never tell what negative energies you may be subjecting yourself to. Very skilled healers can take negative energy and manipulate it into positive, healing energies, but this can be risky. When there is an abundance of other energy sources out there that can be used, I personally don't see the need to use other people's energy in my practices.

• • •

These are just some initial questions you may wish to spend time considering. The more you practise, the more that may arise that you need to work through, especially if you plan to start using healing energy on others. Practice and experience help form the limitations of what we are and are not comfortable with, so keep an open mind as you progress and never be afraid to draw a line where you may be faced with something that crosses your own ethical boundaries.

The Dangers of Energy Work

As we've discussed, energy work is fundamental to our spiritual selves, although it is easy to underestimate the importance of it. We are made of energy and exposed to energy every second of every day whether we like it or not. That energy can have a huge impact on how we feel, the decisions we make, and the actions we take. Even if you aren't actively or consciously partaking in energy work, it is still important to recognise these risks and how to guard against them rather than ignore them. As with most things, prevention is the best cure! There are lots of different ways you can protect yourself from negative energies on a day-to-day basis, which we will get into later in the book. But for now, we will spend a bit of time understanding exactly what it is you might want to protect yourself from.

So, what exactly are the risks? I have split these into two categories. The first category is metaphysical risks; those you could encounter when working with energy itself. Luckily, there aren't many, as energy healing is a relatively safe practice that is open to all.

The second category is those risks you might encounter as an active practitioner in the community, and they have more to do with avoiding scammers and swindlers. As I've mentioned before, there is a lot of information online and there are also a lot of practitioners. Healers, spellcasters, and many others use online communities to share knowledge, meet like-minded people, and promote their businesses. However, as with all communities, there will also be those who try to use these connections to manipulate and scam others out of money, time, and anything else they can get their hands on. Therefore, I have also listed some of the most common scams you may come across within the community, so you can keep your whole self safe as well as your energetical self.

First, let's take a look at those metaphysical dangers. I haven't included how to protect against them or mitigate them, but don't fret—all of that information will be coming later in the book.

An Overabundance of Energy

This can occur when you have taken too much energy into yourself. It can be an uncomfortable feeling and may bring on anxiety in those prone to it, or it may leave you feeling buzzy and restless. You may find it difficult to focus or sleep due to this excess energy. To rid yourself of any excess energy, you need to know how to ground, which essentially allows us to gently and safely rid ourselves of this excess energy.

Lack of Energy

A lack of energy can occur when you have used too much of your own energy and it has left you feeling tired and drained. Most forms of energy healing will stress the importance of connecting to a "universal energy" or external energy source and using this in your healing rather than pulling on your own energy reserves for exactly this reason.

Energy Vampires

Personally, I am not a big fan of the term *energy vampire*, but it is one that most people are familiar with and sums up the situation perfectly. Again, these are people who, whether intentionally or deliberately, "feed" off your energy. Ever been in someone's presence and then afterward just felt drained or out of sorts? This could be attributed to that person feeding off of your energy. Luckily, protection methods such as energy shielding can help prevent this.

External Negative Energy Attacks/Attachments

Remember, energy is neutral, and it is the intention behind it that makes it positive or negative. Some people can give off negative energy without even realising it. The concept of the evil eye is a good example of this; that someone can curse another by casting them a malevolent glare. This is basically just directing negative energy at someone. Think about that boss you have who seems to be constantly stressed and snapping at everyone, or that person who makes snide remarks about you—these are both examples of ways in which people direct negative energy toward you. Whether you are aware of it or not, this negative energy can build up and have a detrimental effect on your overall well-being.

Protecting ourselves from these attacks is the first step, but you also need to know how to rid yourself of any negative energies that may slip through. This is also a very important risk to be aware of if you decide to start practising energy healing, as without the proper knowledge or protections set up, you may find yourself exposed, especially when working with others who may be harbouring a lot of negative energy.

I am involved in quite a few online pagan communities, and one question that crops up a lot from new practitioners is "How do I know if someone has put a curse on me?" In my experience, this is actually quite rare. However, if you do believe that someone is deliberately sending negative energy your way or cursing you, then there are some actions you can perform to protect and cleanse yourself, which we will discuss in chapter 3. In fact, we are more likely to find ourselves a victim of our own negative mindset than someone else's malicious intent, and luckily someone cursing you is probably going to be quite far down on your list of risks to watch out for.

There is another type of energy attack, and that is the otherworldly sort, where some sort of spirit or entity is behind the attack. Again, I wouldn't say this is a regular occurrence or one you need to worry about on a day-to-day basis, but I have experienced it myself. This risk is increased if you are practising astral travel or other workings that involve shifting your consciousness to a different plane, or if you engage in spirit work. However, this is a very unlikely occurrence if you are just practising energy healing. Just like in this world, there are those entities that would intentionally do you harm, and you don't want to let them in or let them attach themselves to you.

Internal Negative Energy Attachments

It is far more likely that any negative energy attachment is one that you have subconsciously created yourself. These are often caused by past trauma you have not properly processed or your own negative self-talk. These can be especially difficult to recognise because often we have lived with them for so long that they just feel like a natural part of us. By connecting with our energy and performing activities such as energy scanning, you can begin to recognise any internal negative energy attachments and then work on ridding yourself of them.

As with all things, there are optimum times to do energy work, and times when you should probably avoid it. If you are performing healing on someone other than yourself, then you need to be a bit stricter about your own state of self. Even with the best protections and cleanses in the world, if you are feeling angry, sad, or any negativity at all then this has the potential to influence your working. This can either weaken your work or potentially infect the other person with this negative energy. Similarly, if you are feeling physically ill, or are in a bad place mentally or emotionally, you may want to avoid performing healing on others; remember, all our states of being are intertwined and any negativity here will also impact your energetic body. Energy healing requires focus and can be hard work, so trying to heal others when you aren't feeling your best also risks impacting your own healing journey and could leave you feeling worse.

If you are performing healing for yourself, chances are that you will be performing it to help you overcome these difficulties and manage this negativity. In these instances, it is permissible to perform energy work on yourself in these states. Just ensure that you are able to disconnect from your troubles and trust that they won't impede your ability to connect with and work with healing energies.

Practitioner Dangers

Now, let's look at those dangers you may face more generally as a practitioner. This isn't just limited to energy work; anybody who practises any sort of spiritual activity should be aware of these and seek to avoid them, whether that is in online communities or in-person communities. It can be difficult to determine who is genuine and who isn't, and the below guidance is built upon my own experiences within communities, and those with whom I also trust within those communities.

The Fakers

The fakers are those who are in it for show; they tout a wide range of titles. Titles can often show a practitioner's experience, but they can also be bought quite easily online. The information that they share will often be very basic beginner information or taken from other people's social media accounts, books. Very rarely do they talk about their own experiences. These people crave status, and you will often find little substance to what they communicate.

The Takers

The takers are people who have integrated themselves into the community because they want something from it; whether that's money, business, adoration, time, or anything else they can get. Most of their interactions are very complimentary but ultimately result in them trying to sell you something or ask for favours. Any help they do give you will often come with a catch. There is nothing wrong with interacting with these people if they are legitimate and are just trying to run their business. But ensure that you understand these sorts of relationships are purely transactional and do not get too sucked in.

The Untruthful

The untruthful are the people who will tell you that you definitely have a generational curse attached to you, that you have a lot of negativity surrounding you, or similar. This will usually take place extremely early in the conversation. They will exaggerate their experience greatly. Often there is a monetary angle to it; they can remove the curse for a fee for example. One evening I received a direct message (DM) on Instagram from someone who said they felt drawn to my energy and to give me a reading (for a price, of course). I always ignore these messages, as I tend to receive a lot of them, but that evening I decided to play along out of curiosity.

After paying an extortionate fee, they came back to me roughly three minutes later with my tarot reading. This was the first red flag; it doesn't matter how experienced you are, there is no way you can connect with your guides, perform a reading, interpret it, and write it all out in a message in three minutes. Of course, the reading revealed that I had a curse placed on me by a relative who was jealous of my potential success, which the practitioner could also remove for a fee. Needless to say, I stopped engaging with them at that point.

The "Pioneers"

Often the pioneers are people pushing and advertising their own method of healing that they devised themselves or that was "revealed" to them during meditation by a 100-year-old guru atop a mountain in the astral realm. Most of the time when you drill down into the detail of what they are offering, it is absolutely nothing new, just a repackaging of a well-established system. Often, they will want to charge you a lot of money for this "secret knowledge" too. I do believe that there is no right way to perform energy healing, and there may be systems yet undiscovered that could greatly benefit a wide range of people. However, it is all too easy for someone to appropriate an already well-known system and try to sell it as a miracle cure.

The Money Chasers

It's all about the money with the money chasers. They sell easy courses (a lot of them) in several different (often unrelated) healing methods, and these can be pricey! They sell oils, crystals, jewellery, crystal-infused water bottles, machines that will protect you from 5G … the list goes on. Apart from selling these products, they don't really have much else to offer the community. Their social media is just them flogging their wares or messaging everyone they come across to advertise their services. Otherwise, they have very little interaction with the community, and they tend to just regurgitate well-known, beginner information.

So how can you tell if someone is legitimate? The following actions won't 100 percent protect you from getting scammed—scammers are extremely clever—but it should drastically improve your chances of avoiding them whether online or in person.

- Talk to friends and others in the community to get recommendations on sources they have used and can vouch for the legitimacy of said sources.
- Check reviews and who is giving those reviews. Are they all from real people? Any review that has come from an account that has no other activity than writing that one review is automatically suspicious.
- Check how much they are charging for products and services compared to others in their field. Beware of any price that is so cheap it feels too good to be true (it usually is) or any that is astronomically high compared to the market average.
- Check out their payment methods. Most scammers will avoid any sort of payment platform that will allow you to raise a refund request if you aren't happy with their service.
- Know what you want and don't let yourself be talked into anything else, at least without verifying it with someone you trust first. If you ask a reiki healer for one session and they tell you that you will need at least five before you are unblocked, try and get a second opinion.
- Never spend more money than you have. Similar to above, make a budget and stick with it, not allowing yourself to be talked into spending more than you can afford.
- Research any claims or statements made by practitioners, either in regard to their services or the products they are selling. If it sounds suspicious, untrue, too good to be true, or verging on conspiracy theory territory, take a step back and look elsewhere.

- Avoid anyone who messages you directly, especially privately on social media. Ignore messages if they say anything along the lines of "I was drawn to your profile" or "my guides told me I had to message you." A lot of the time these messages will make it sound like there is some fate-decided reason as to why you two should connect but trust me when I say that by the time you receive that message, they have already sent it to fifty other people that day.

Chapter One Reflections

This is your chance to start thinking about what energy work means to you and why you want to master it. Take your journal and spend some time considering the information in this initial chapter as well as answer the questions below. I always find it interesting to come back to this once you have been practising for a few months and see how your perception has changed (if it has). I know you may be keen to rush ahead and get to the more practical exercises, but this is always a good starting point to make sure you fully understand the foundations of the work you are about to embark on.

1. What is your own personal definition of energy?
2. Why is practising energy work important, and why do you want to practise it?
3. From an ethical point of view, what is your opinion on karmic consequences?
4. From an ethical point of view, would you send healing energy to someone without their permissions? Why or why not?
5. Think about your day-to-day life; what are the most common dangers, or sources of negative energy, you think you might encounter?

CHAPTER TWO

Connecting with Energy

You've made it through the theory, which means now we can get to the fun part—the doing!

As with all new skills, do not worry if you don't pick it up straight away or if you don't feel anything the first time you try any of these exercises. Whilst energy is natural and is all around us, oftentimes we have closed ourselves off to it. We are taught to rely on our physical senses to interpret the world around us and ignore our intuition and any other sense that cannot be empirically verified. Unfortunately, there isn't a switch we can flick on and immediately be able to start sensing this energy. As is the way when learning any new skill, it is advised to start small, try several different approaches, and determine what personally works for you. There are many different ways that people experience energy, which will impact how you work with it. So, if one of these exercises isn't working for you, try different ones until you find one that does.

You may also be wondering how often you should be performing these exercises. My go-to answer is: as often as you feel they need to be done (I'm sorry, I appreciate that is quite a vague answer). A lot of practitioners recommend performing these exercises daily, but for many (including myself) that can be unrealistic. You may find that the more adept you become at these techniques and the more self-aware you become through your practice, the less you will need to do them. As always, find a routine that works for you. There is a whole section further on in this book that is centred around building a sustainable practice, so do not fret about the frequency you should be performing these exercises just yet.

The first thing to understand before we move forward, and it is a point I have already mentioned several times, is that everyone experiences energy differently because people vibrate at different frequencies. You may simply feel energy, often at that vibrational level or through physical cues such as your hair standing on end. You may actually see energy as colours, light, patterns, and so forth. You may get pictures or words that pop into your mind, or you may even hear sounds. You may find it is a combination of several of these, and it can often depend on the energy you are working with and how you are working with it.

In this chapter, we will first focus on creating the space within ourselves to be able to start sensing energy, and for that we will be using meditation. We tend to experience the world around us through our five physical senses: sight, touch, taste, smell, and hearing. However, energy is much more of a subtle force, and it can be difficult to recognise it or connect with it when our minds are being bombarded every second with the information being fed to us through those five senses. Meditation allows us to take a break from these constant inputs and instead focus our attention on the subtle force that is energy.

Then we will turn our attention to grounding and centring, which will help us to connect with the present moment and introduce us to exercises we can use to help us draw energy into ourselves. We will look at finding our power centre, through which we can start to feel how energy flows throughout our own body and use this as a place of power when we begin to practice healing.

This exercise sets us up nicely to move into breathwork, where we begin to explore that energy flow and the effect it has on us, as well as how our breath directly affects that flow of energy within us. Finally, we move on to creating energy orbs and sensing the energy of different crystals. Both exercises are designed to help you start feeling the energy outside of yourself. This will allow you to start focusing on controlling that energy and using it in your working.

At the end of this chapter, I will provide several journal prompts to help you record your experiences with each exercise, so make sure you keep that journal handy!

Meditation

Meditation is an ancient art, and one that is not just beneficial to energy work. There are many reasons to practise meditation. It can help us control our thoughts, feelings, and emotions. It can help us be more present in the moment. It can help us focus and bring us insight and clarity by allowing us to connect with our subconscious.

These skills will greatly improve your ability to connect with and control your energetic self and the energy around you. When we encounter negative energy or find ourselves in toxic situations, meditation can aid us in being able to distance ourselves from the negative side effects of that energy—unwelcome thoughts, feeling sad, lonely, angry—and instead focus on strengthening our protections. Meditation can also help us block out the everyday humdrum that can distract us and allow us to travel within ourselves and connect with our energy more easily. This will be key for many of the exercises later in this book.

So, whilst meditation isn't an exercise that is mutually exclusive to energy work, it is an exercise that will greatly enhance your ability to establish and work with that energetic connection.

I have found that little and often is the most effective approach with meditation. The majority of people will say that practising for five minutes a day has allowed them to master the art of meditation much better than an hour-long meditation session once a week.

There are so many apps out there that will guide you in meditation, as well as classes, recorded guided meditations, and books on the subject. However, as useful as these tools are, you don't need them to get started. All you need is yourself and somewhere quiet where you won't be disturbed for a few minutes. It may sound simple, but meditation can be surprisingly difficult. Our brains aren't used to being ignored or switched off, and at first you may find your mind actively working against you, desperate to remind you that you need to throw the expired milk away, or of that embarrassing childhood moment you haven't thought about in years. So, as with all exercises in this book, do not feel disheartened if something that sounds so easy in theory is actually quite difficult in practise.

Comfort is key in meditation, and most people prefer to sit or lie down when meditating. If you are sitting, I find that sitting on a couple of thick cushions so my hips are raised above my knees is a much more comfortable position to maintain for a longer period of time than just sitting directly on the floor.

I personally love listening to music when I'm meditating, as it helps me block out other distractions. However, others find the music distracting, so it is up to you if you wish to listen to music or not. If you do decide to include music, choose songs that are similar or have a simplistic beat and continuous rhythm so you aren't suddenly pulled from your meditation by an unexpected tempo change.

You may also wish to burn incense or certain oils to aid you. There are several scents that are associated with peace, relaxation, and helping our mind to settle so it is more accepting of the stillness we are trying to create. Lavender, chamomile, and rosemary are all great scents to start off with.

Beginner's Meditation Exercise

Find a comfortable position, close your eyes, and take at least three deep breaths, inhaling through the nose and exhaling through the mouth. Clear your mind and focus on nothing but your breath.

We are going to continue this, but we are going to count with the breath. As you inhale, count "one" in your head. As you exhale, count "two" in your head. On the next inhale, count "three," and on the exhale count "four." Continue counting your breaths, one for the inhale and one for the exhale, until you reach ten. Then, go back to the beginning and start with "one" and carry on until you reach ten again.

As you breathe in, follow the breath as it flows down into you, through your throat, down through your ribcage, and into your diaphragm. See it collecting at the bottom of your diaphragm. As you exhale, feel this breath travelling back up your torso and out through your mouth. Focus on this flow of breath with each count.

As you breathe, chances are thoughts are going to float into your head. You will wonder if you remembered to turn the oven off, you will remember that you need to send that email, and you will start to wonder what you should have for dinner. Remember, our brains aren't used to being told to turn off and just focus on one thought for a prolonged period of time. Don't stress when this occurs. Instead, we will practise something often recommended for beginners called noting; simply recognise the thought, acknowledge it (or "note it"), and then let it go and come back to your breathing.

Continue this exercise for as long as feels comfortable. When you feel ready, bring your awareness back to the present moment by wiggling your fingers and toes. Slowly open your eyes.

The exercise may sound simple, but it can be surprising how difficult, and maybe even frustrating, it can feel at first. However, you will also be surprised at how quickly your mind will adapt to it with consistent practice. I've been practising meditation for many years and can honestly say it has had a hugely positive impact on my day-to-day health and well-being, not just my spiritual practice, and it is one I will recommend to anyone.

Grounding and Centring

Grounding is the art of connecting with the environment around us to bring ourselves stability, feel more present in the moment, and help rid ourselves of negative or excess energies. Many people prefer to use the element of earth for this; it is the earth that we are anchored to, and it is generally associated with stability and strong foundations. Think of it like the earth wire in a plug, helping to protect against "electric shocks" (or in this case the negative effects of excess or negative energies). However, you can use the other elements to help you ground.

I personally focus on the waters that run beneath the earth's surface and anchor to those, as I feel more of an affinity with the element of water. You could think of the fiery, molten core at the centre of the earth and use that to aid you in grounding if you feel more of an affinity with the fire element.

Centring is the art of being able to bring the energies within yourself into balance, to help yourself feel more focused and together. Grounding and centring often go hand-in-hand, first grounding, and then centring. However, you can just do one or the other if needed.

Grounding and centring are often considered fundamental in practising energy work, and they can also help maintain our health and well-being on a day-to-day basis. It can aid you in cleansing yourself of negative energies, feel more focused and in control, and help you better control and direct energy.

There are many different ways to ground and centre, but the following exercises are the ones that resonate most for me. They are quite popular methods, so you may have come across them before, but that is because they are so effective. Simply type "grounding roots meditation" into any search engine and you will see hundreds of websites, videos, and blogs explaining how to do it. Below is my own version of this grounding exercise.

Whilst there seems to be a difference of opinion on which should come first—grounding or centring—I personally recommend starting off with grounding and then moving on to centring.

Grounding—Roots Meditation

With feet on the floor, prepare as if you were going into meditation. This might involve taking some deep breaths, putting on some music, or similar.

When you feel ready, feel your feet against the ground. Wriggle your toes, and really get a sense of how your feet feel pressed against the ground.

Now visualise roots growing from your feet. You may see these as the roots of a plant, you may see these as tendrils of light, or you may visualise something completely different. Again, as someone who feels an affinity with the element of water, I tend to visualise them as bladderwrack, or seaweed, stretching down. These roots will connect you to the earth and allow energy to pass both to you and from you.

See the roots from your feet plunging into the ground. See them pushing down through the soil, spreading out, and winding around the natural debris that lies beneath the earth. Feel that connection to the earth, to the universal energy that is present in all things.

Once you feel these roots anchoring you to the earth, visualise all the excess energy from within you flowing out through your body. It travels down, through your feet, out through your roots, and into the earth. I like to visualise it as a white light that starts at the top of my head and pushes down through my body, forcing any excess energy out through my roots. You may see it as a different coloured light, or you may not see a light at all but just feel the energy leaving your body. Some people like to visualise a waterfall of light tumbling down from above their heads, through their body, and washing away all the excess energy into the earth. Whatever imagery you prefer to use, trust that this energy will reach the earth and dissipate, leaving us feeling calm, present, and grounded.

It may take a few minutes before you feel the effect of this exercise, but the more regularly you do it, the quicker you will be able to achieve it.

Centring—Roots Extended

This is an extension of our grounding meditation. To start, follow the steps outlined for the roots meditation until you have visualised the roots coming from your feet and anchoring you into the ground.

Next, we will visualise roots again, but this time they extend from the crown of your head and up into the sky, reaching up as they spiral toward the heavens. They pass the tallest trees and towers, up through the clouds, through the outer layers of our atmosphere and anchor you to the world above. As the adage goes, "as above, so below."

Now, visualise the energy coming from the earth, travelling up through the roots of your lower half, and into the centre of your body. At the same time, visualise the energy from the skies travelling down the roots from your crown and into the centre of your body. I find that focusing on this pull of energy on the inhale and then releasing on the exhale works well. See this energy meeting in the middle of your body and joining. You are perfectly balanced in the centre of this energy, connected to both the earth and the skies, the perfect point between above and below. Continue this exercise until you feel this sense of balance within yourself.

Finding Your Power Centre

This next exercise is possibly the most important one to master before you progress, and this is to find your own power centre.

The power centre is the seat of your power. It is where you can connect best with your energy, draw energy into yourself to heal from, and use that energy to manifest out into the world. When we centre by using the previous exercise, it is often our power centre we are centring into.

Most pinpoint the power centre as being the solar plexus chakra, which sits just below the rib cage—more on chakras in chapter 4. However, in my experience, it is different for everyone. I personally feel my power centre covers the solar plexus chakra and up into the centre of my rib cage. You may feel you best connect with your power centre from the third eye or brow region. In Usui Reiki, this point is called the *hara* and is found in your lower belly, beneath your navel.[5] As always, it is best to discover what works for you, as what will strengthen your practice the most is understanding how you best interact with energy.

I have found that the centring exercises are great for understanding exactly where your power centre is. You can use the roots exercise and note where in your body you feel the energy of the earth and sky joining in your body, but I personally find that the next meditation is more effective in helping you establish where the seat of your inner power is.

The Calming Seas Centring Method

Find somewhere quiet where you won't be disturbed and you can sit peacefully. Close your eyes, take a few deep breaths, and spend a few moments clearing your mind of all thoughts.

Bring your attention inward, to the centre of your body, and visualise yourself sitting on a large, flat rock in the middle of an endless ocean. Observe the waves; are they large, wild, crashing around you, or are they relatively calm? This will give an indication as to your inner state and how centred you currently are.

We want to focus on calming the waves as much as possible. Take a deep breath in and see the waves being drawn to you. As you exhale, see the waves flowing back into the sea, calmer than before. Inhale again and see the waves rolling toward you, and then exhale, again focusing on breathing calming energies into the waves.

As you do this, note exactly where in your body it feels as though you are pulling the waves into. This is your power centre.

Continue this and see the waves settling until you find yourself in the centre of calm, still waters, perfectly centred and balanced.

I will stress again that this is the most important exercise you should feel comfortable performing before you continue with energy

5. Mikao Usui and Frank Arjava Petter, *The Original Reiki Handbook of Dr. Mikao Usui: The Traditional Usui Reiki Ryoho Treatment Positions and Numerous Reiki Techniques for Health and Well-Being* (Lotus Press, 1999), Kindle.

work. Do not fret if you do not get it straight away because, as with anything, it can take practice. To some, it may come naturally, but do not be put off if it doesn't work the first, the second, or even the third time. Try to spend a few minutes each day practising; you will find that the more you practise, the easier it will become, and before long, you will be able to connect with it instantly whenever and wherever you are without the need to consciously practise it.

Breathwork

In Sanskrit, the word *prana* means "breath, life force, or vital principle (of life)." As with most of the information in this book, it is a complex subject, and a lot has been written about it.

There are several different meanings or understandings of prana, from physical breath to the energy that comprises our consciousness. However, the simplest way to explain it is that prana is this universal energy, or life force. Our breath is the most direct way in which we experience and interact with prana, and so breathwork is a great starting point to help us connect with and feel our own energy.

Here are four of the most common breathing techniques. Don't be surprised if you find these more difficult than you expected (I did when I first started practising them). Even for something as natural as breathing that we do unconsciously every day, mastering something new takes a bit of effort. You can do these exercises either sitting down or standing up. It is recommended not to try these exercises lying down, as you won't be able to take in the required amount of oxygen to sustain your breaths.

As you perform these exercises, try to clear your mind and focus on nothing but your breath, as we do when meditating. Feel it entering your body, moving through you, and then exiting your body as you exhale. You may wish to focus on just feeling this flow of breath, or you may wish to visualise your breath as a white light flowing into, through you, and out of you. Or maybe you hear the energy—perhaps it makes different sounds or notes as it moves through you.

Once you have finished each breathing exercise, reflect on how you feel. Do you feel any different from before you started? Maybe you feel more balanced, more relaxed, or maybe more energised depending on the breath? Pay attention and really consider every aspect of this connection, and make sure you record your experiences in your journal.

The Vase Breath

The vase breath is one of the most common and one of the easiest breaths to master. You should feel comfortable maintaining this breath before moving on to any of the other breathing exercises listed here.

Before you begin, take note of your breathing—this can be difficult when you are aware of what you are about to do, as you may find that you subconsciously start trying to control it. Try to catch yourself unaware at some point beforehand. Many people will notice that they take rather short, shallow breaths, mostly focused in the chest area. With this breath we will be focusing on taking deeper, more balanced breaths into the abdomen, which should allow us to take in more air.

Focus on inhaling through your nose and exhaling back out through your nose rather than your mouth. You also need to make sure your inhale and exhale are of equal length; for example, either four, five, or six counts in and the same amount out.

Once you feel settled, focus on pulling all of your breath into your stomach, expanding it outward to hold all the oxygen you are taking in. At the end of your count, exhale and, as you reach the end of your breath, suck in your stomach and force yourself to expel any remaining stale air before you start again. Continue in this manner for as long as you want. Remember to keep the length of your inhale and exhale equal and try not to hold your breath at any point; let it flow in a continuous cycle.

You should find that you feel yourself taking in more air, helping you take longer and deeper breaths. This is a good one to practise when you are feeling anxious or nervous about something and to generally help your body feel the benefits of taking in more oxygen.

The Three-Part Breath

The three-part breath is similar to the vase breath, but it has a couple of extra steps. First, perform the vase breath, but rather than focusing on keeping all of your breath just in your abdomen, fill up this area first before filling your chest and then your throat. You are filling yourself with air from the bottom up.

As you exhale, focus on first expelling the air from your throat, then your lungs, and then your abdomen. Some recommend that you place one hand on your abdomen and one hand on your chest to help you focus. I find that it helps to mentally visualise yourself as the vase with three separate sections, and your breath is the water being poured into the vase. Once the bottom section (your abdomen) is full, the water fills the middle section (your chest), and once this is full, the top section (your throat).

Repeat this breath for as long as you feel comfortable. Remember to try and keep your inhale and exhale breaths of the same length.

Nine Breaths of Purification

This one is great for helping you balance yourself if you are feeling a bit out of sorts, to "clear the cobwebs." In Pranayama, we are taught that there are three main energy channels within the body—the centre, the left, and the right channels—and this breathing technique is designed to help clear them. It can also help unblock your sinuses when you are suffering from a cold. As such, even if you aren't suffering from a cold, it can sometimes cause a bit of a runny nose, so it is best to have some tissues at hand just in case!

To perform this breath, start with the vase breath. Once you feel ready, raise your dominant hand so you are holding it in front of your face and place your index, middle, and ring fingers on the top of your nose. Cover one of your nostrils using your thumb/little finger and inhale through your one open nostril. Now, use your thumb/little finger (whichever one you have not yet used) to block the nostril you have inhaled from at the same time you release the nostril you formally had closed, and then exhale through your now open nostril.

Once you have exhaled fully, inhale through this same nostril. Now swap as you did before so you close that nostril and open the other before exhaling. Finally, release both nostrils, and inhale and exhale through both nostrils.

You should find yourself in a pattern of exhaling and inhaling through one nostril, then exhaling and inhaling through the other, and then through both. This should be completed nine times.

The Lion's Breath

This breath is good for encouraging release, although it is probably not one to practise in public unless you want to receive some funny looks!

Start with the vase breath to settle yourself and your breathing. When you feel ready, inhale as usual and then tilt your head back, open your mouth wide, stick your tongue out, and exhale loudly through the mouth. Inhale again as you would with the vase breath, tilting your head forward and exhaling in the same fashion. You can also try raising your arms as you exhale to emphasise the release effect.

Energy Orbs

So far, we have focused on feeling energy on a more personal level, the energy within us. Energy orbs are a great practice to help you get a feel for energy external to us, which will provide a great foundation for practising energy healing. Plus, it's a lot of fun.

I've read about this exercise in many books, I've practised it as a part of a coven, and it was even taught as a part of my reiki training. It is a common exercise, but again, that is because it is so effective.

Through this exercise, we also get our first taste of taking energy from our external environment and using that in our energy work as opposed to using our internal energy supply. This is a key skill in energy healing, and one that is used later on in the book as a part of other exercises, so it is definitely worth ensuring you feel comfortable with this particular one before moving on.

Creating an Energy Orb

The best way to start is to first rub your hands together. Give them a good rub and feel the energy building.

Now, pull your hands apart slowly, until they are a short distance from each other. You should still be able to feel the energy between your hands. Again, you may physically feel it, hear it buzz, see it as a glowing light, or you may have a different experience—as I keep emphasising, everyone experiences energy differently and it is up to you to discover how you do so.

Now play with it. Move your hands farther apart and feel it thin, push them together and feel the energy condense. Twist and twirl it around your palms and have fun with it. When I was a part of a coven, we would do this and pass the orbs to one another—you can really feel the energy as you pass it from one person to the other.

You can also focus on making this energy orb grow by adding more energy to it. To do this, we can employ the techniques we have already learned about in this book and amend them slightly, so we are now taking the energy from our external environment rather than using our own energy. One way to do this is to use the roots and antlers meditation; however, rather than focusing on sending your excess energy down your roots and out of yourself, visualise instead pulling energy from the earth. See this energy travelling up through your roots, through your feet, then rising up through your body, down your arms, and out through your palms and into your energy orb. Or you might want to use the roots meditation to the same effect, focusing on taking the energy from the earth and the sky. Finally, you may wish to use the breathwork; as you inhale, see yourself breathing in the energy around you and funnelling this through your body, down your arms, and out through your palms.

Advanced Energy Orbs

Energy orbs have many uses and can help you manifest specific intentions, which can be very beneficial in healing. For example, if you are suffering from an ache in a particular part of your body, you could create your orb and infuse it with the intention of healing.

To infuse is very simple; focus on your intent as you create your orb and see this intention being transferred into it. I personally associated the colour green with healing, so I would focus on the word *healing* as I am creating my orb and see my energy orb as a glowing green colour.

Let's say for example that you are struggling with your confidence or you lack self-esteem. You could create your orb and focus on the intent of "confidence," whilst visualising a bright yellow or gold colour (both associated with confidence) orb. Then use your hands to push the orb into your solar plexus chakra (the chakra of the body associated with your personal power).

You can also use energy orbs to create a shield around other objects. To do so, create your energy orb, infuse it with your intention, and then place the orb around your chosen object. See this object surrounded by the orb, being empowered by its energy and its intent. This is especially useful if you wish to empower a crystal, items of jewellery, and other items to bring you healing.

Energy orbs are a great way of learning how to connect with and control the energy around you. It is an extremely useful technique that will aid you in many of the energy healing methods we will discuss later in the book. I highly recommend you take the time to practise this particular exercise until you feel confident you can sense the energy.

Sensing Energy of Other Things

The whole universe is composed of energy, and so everything has an energetic vibration. Animals, plants, and even inanimate objects also have this vibration. The more complex the organism, the more complex the energy surrounding it will be. I have also found that natural objects have a stronger vibration than man-made or "unnatural" objects.

Connecting with this energy is a great way to learn more about an object. You can connect with the energy of other people as well as objects. You may have heard the term *empath* before. Those who identify as empaths naturally connect with the energy of other people, and through that what they are thinking and feeling, to the point where it feels as though they themselves are experiencing those feelings and emotions. It is especially important for empaths to be able to protect and shield themselves from others' energy, as this can become overwhelming, especially if they are surrounded by people who harbour quite negative energies.

This works for animals, plants, trees, and other natural constructs also. You can connect with the energy of a sick tree to find out what it needs to heal it, or connect with the energy of an animal to understand if it is content with its environment.

You may have also heard of psychometry, or the ability to connect with an object and get impressions from it—of its previous owners, where it's been, and what it's seen. This is done through connecting with the energy of an object by reading its energetic imprint.

Finally, we can borrow the energy of objects to aid us in our workings. When we use crystals, herbs, and such, we are using their energy to fuel our intent and add power to our workings. We can directly pull on this energy to fuse it with our own, or to use it instead of our own when we are healing or manifesting.

Crystal Energy Exercise

A great way to begin your work into sensing different external energies is working with crystals. Crystals are fantastic little bundles of energy, and different types of crystals will vibrate at completely different frequencies and have different energetic associations.

For this exercise, choose at least three very different crystals. Find somewhere comfortable to sit and place the three crystals in front of you. Clear your mind and focus on your intent; you are here to read the energy of these crystals.

Pick up the first crystal and focus on connecting with its energy. I find it helps to visualise the energy field around the crystal like a force field and then hold my hand over the crystal and visualise my own personal energy intermingling with the crystal's energy. Then, just listen and pay attention to whatever comes into your mind. Does the energy feel light or heavy? Is it buzzy or quite slow and dull? Do you get any specific emotions from it? Do any words pop into your head, any colours, or do you hear any sounds? Don't fight these; just let them come to you. Once you are done, write down your impressions from the crystal.

Clear your mind and repeat the process with your second crystal and then your third crystal. Then reflect on your impressions. How did they differ? Were there any similarities, or did you notice any trends or patterns in the way you sensed the energy? How did each one make you feel after you put the crystal down?

Another interesting exercise is to use the crystals and then try the exercise with a piece of glass. Glass has a noticeably different vibration and is a good object to include just so you can really feel the difference.

Once you have mastered this, try working with two crystals at once and feeling their combined energy. Imagine it as if you were mixing paint; mix blue and yellow together and you get green, a whole new colour. Combining the energy of two crystals will, in most cases, produce a new or different energy. In some cases, these two energies just won't gel. For example, I find that combining selenite and rose quartz creates a really powerful, loving healing energy. But combining hematite and rose quartz creates an emotional block sort of feeling, and rather than helping us explore our emotions, it stops us from feeling them altogether. This is not necessarily a bad thing and could be useful for some people, but for me, it feels quite avoidant and always makes me feel a little uneasy.

Now, one thing to mention here is that we are focusing on just feeling the energy of the crystals; we aren't focusing on taking those energies into ourselves. This is an important distinction to make. We don't want to be letting this energy in before we have sussed out whether it is positive, negative, or neutral. It's akin to hearing a knock on the door and opening it without checking who's there. Most of the time it will probably be fine, but if it isn't... well, things can go very wrong! Once you have connected with this energy and determined it isn't negative, you can go ahead and use it in your workings. There will be more information on using crystals specifically for healing later in the book.

Chapter Two Reflections

In this chapter, we have engaged with several different practices that are built around helping us connect with our own energy, and the energy in the world around us. Whilst they aren't energy healing techniques themselves, they are considered fundamental practices that will aid you greatly in your healing journey.

1. How easy/difficult did you find the grounding and centring exercises? Did you feel different after performing them than you did before?
2. Where is your power centre located? How did it feel when you were drawing energy into this area?

3. How did you feel when performing any of the breathing exercises? Did they have different effects on you? Did you feel any different before you tried it compared to afterward?
4. How did you personally experience the energy when performing the energy orb exercise—did you feel it, see it, experience any sort of colours, words, or other sensations as you did it?
5. Could you feel any difference in the energy of each crystal when practising the crystal energy exercise, and if so, what were those differences?

CHAPTER THREE

Hygiene and Best Practise

As we have discussed, energy is fluid, and our personal energy is very susceptible to the energy of others and our environment. To ensure we are keeping our own energy as healthy as possible, it is important to practise good hygiene. In the same way we shower and brush our teeth to keep our physical bodies clean, we can also keep our energetic bodies clean through practices commonly referred to as cleansing. Cleansing is the act of removing these negative energies, and there are several ways we can do this.

I am a big proponent of prevention being better than cure, especially when it comes to energy work. Whilst we need to know how to cleanse ourselves of these negative energies once we have picked them up, it is better if we just don't pick them up at all. Unfortunately, it is difficult to completely avoid places, people, or situations where this negativity can arise. Learning how to protect ourselves from that energy is a core skill that every energy practitioner should try to become proficient in. Doing so will stop you from absorbing those negative energies and protect you from those that would drain your energy.

As with everything we have discussed so far, there are many different methods of cleansing and protection. Some you may find easier than others, and some more effective than others. First, we will look at some of the key methods of protection before we move on to cleansing.

Protection

For those who are new to protection, I highly recommend energy shields. These are especially useful if you want to protect yourself from others' energy or prevent them from feeding off of your own energy. It is one of the most effective forms of protection out there and can be done as and when you need it with no additional tools. However, don't let that stop you from trying any others. If you are looking for immediate protection, then maybe one of the other methods may help you with that "quick fix" while you practise shielding.

Energy Shields

The idea behind energy shielding is to manipulate energy to cast a bubble, or a shield, around you, which nothing can break through. Whilst this is definitely a very effective method, you do need to recharge your energy shield regularly for it to work.

How often you need to recharge it depends on how often you feel it will need to be used, and also how familiar you are with the practice. If you find that there aren't many situations where you could find yourself exposed to negative energy, you may just focus on building your shield as and when you need it. If you are regularly exposed to this energy—maybe through a toxic work environment, for example—you may want to recharge it every morning. Similarly, the more adept you are at this practice, the less you may feel the need to recharge your shield, as you can sustain it for longer. When you are first starting out, you may feel your shield is weaker and needs recharging more often.

There are two common approaches to creating energy shields. The first is to use the energy within you and expand it out; the second is to use the universal energy around you and pull it in to create the shield. I personally recommend the latter. I have always found that using my internal energy for this exercise is draining to the point it will give me a headache, and my shield never feels as strong. I will cover both approaches for you to experiment with and determine your preferred way of working, but I will always recommend using universal energy for any "outward" working.

Building Your Energy Shield

To use your own energy to create this energy shield, first ground and centre, and then find your power centre. Once you have completed this initial step, focus on your breathing, as we will be using this to control the energy in order to build our shield.

As you inhale, focus on pulling the energy within your body into your power centre. As you exhale, focus on pushing this energy out around your body. Feel it building within you, coursing around your body. Perform this part of the exercise for a few breaths until you feel comfortable with it and can feel the energy within you.

When you feel ready, we will take it one step further on the exhale. As you breathe out, focus on pushing this energy out through your skin. See, or feel, it form a bubble or a skinsuit around you, a protective shield that has the intention of blocking any negative energies out. Generally, when creating energy shields, we visualise a perfectly rounded bubble surrounding us, but you may find it easier to see the energy outlining the shape of your body. This energy frames your head, your shoulders, and down your body to the tips of your toes. You can keep this shape, or you can further expand it into the traditional bubble shape if you prefer.

If you would prefer to use universal energy to create your energy shield (which again I recommend), we will use the same approach that we took for creating our energy orbs. Using either the roots meditation or the breathwork exercises, draw energy from the external environment into yourself. Gather this energy in your power centre and then push it out through your body to form the shield.

When you are more experienced at shielding, you won't even need to take this energy into yourself first; you will be able to pull this energy directly into your shield. See, or feel, the energy swirling around you, encompassing you to create your energy shield, a protective bubble that will keep you safe from any negative energies you may encounter.

Once I feel as though I have enough energy to maintain my shield, I like to say a simple affirmation to confirm my intent and effectively close the exercise, such as: "This shield is cast, and I am protected."

Once you have created your shield, you can finish the exercise and trust that your shield will protect you as you go about your day-to-day business. If at any point you feel that you need to strengthen your shield, see it in your mind's eye and use any one of the methods you just learned to add more energy to it.

Advanced Energy Shielding

Once you are adept at casting this basic energy shield, you may wish to experiment with different types of energy shields. Below are some suggestions as to more advanced shielding techniques you may wish to try.

Programming Your Shield to Absorb Negative Energy

You might want to try programming your shield to manage negative energies in a specific way. My personal favourite is to create a shield that will absorb any negative energy it picks up and transform it into positive energy, which is then used to strengthen the shield further. To do this, I work with the element of water to create my shield, as this element is associated with transformation.

I am lucky enough to live near a river, so I will sit facing the river and instead of drawing energy from the earth or from above, I draw the energy from the river using the same approach. If you do not have access to a large body of water, you could use a large bowl of water or even rainfall if, like me, you live in a country known for its rainy weather!

Visualise your shield as crashing waves encompassing you, wrapping around you. See negative energy approaching you; I tend to visualise it as tiny black pellets flying toward my shield. Then, see the waves of your shield catching this negativity and transforming it into positive energy as the waters flow. This is now positive energy further strengthening your shield.

Shielding Against Deliberate Energy Attacks

If you believe that someone is deliberately directing negative energy your way, you may wish to create a "return to sender" shield that will reflect that negative energy back toward the person sending it. To do this, visualise your shield as a mirror. See those negative energies bouncing off the reflective surface of this mirror and back toward its source.

Whilst this type of shield can feel appropriate if you know there is somebody who is deliberately and maliciously sending negative energy your way, again consider the ethics of energy work. Maybe someone is unconsciously sending negative energy out. Maybe they are going through a difficult period in their life and are resentful toward your successes, or jealous that perhaps you seem better off than them in that moment. Is it really fair to send this negative energy back to them if it is unintentionally sent, borne out of an individual's already desperate mental state? As with most of these ethical conundrums, there is no wrong or right answer, and only you can set your own boundaries in accordance with your own moral code.

The Double-Layered Shield

This shield is ideal if you know you are going to be surrounded by intense negative energy, or if you believe that someone is deliberately sending negative energy your way. To create this shield, we will be visualising two shields around us.

Perform the roots meditation to the point where you have extended roots out from both your feet and your head. First, focus on drawing the energy up through the earth and creating your initial shield. See this shield spinning or flowing around you in a clockwise direction.

Once you feel confident that this first shield is strong and sustainable, focus on drawing energy down from the sky. Use this energy to build a second shield over the top of your first shield. You want to visualise this shield spinning or flowing in a counterclockwise direction, in contrast with your first shield.

Once you have built both layers of your shield, spend a bit of time focusing on drawing the energy up through your foot and down through your head. Feed this energy into both layers of your shield simultaneously. If any negative energy should get through the first layer of your shield, then the shields' opposing movements should see that negative energy get stuck before it has the chance to penetrate the second layer of your shield.

This is a technique that I have had great success with, and although it does require an extra level of focus, I urge you to give it a go in those extreme circumstances where you may need it.

Symbols of Protection

A symbol is a pictorial representation of a person's intent. You can use well-known symbols associated with protection, or you can create your own. Whichever you decide to use will depend on your personal preference. The plus side of using a well-known symbol is that it is already defined and, having been long associated with protection, will make it easier to connect with that intent. However, building your own will leave you with a more personalised symbol, one that is imbued with your own energy, strengthening your connection with it.

If you wish to use a symbol known for protection, you could use the Christian cross or the equal-armed cross. The Eye of Horus is commonly used to ward off harm. You could also use the Hamsa, a symbol used to protect against the evil eye.

There are many different approaches to making your own symbol. You could use one of the symbols just mentioned as a basis for creating your own. If you work with planetary energy, you could use the magic square associated with Jupiter, a planet associated with protection. If you wish to create your own, then rest assured that I discuss working with the energy of the planets later in the book. This includes listing the magic squares associated with each planet and instructions on how to use them to create symbols.

There are many ways you can use your chosen symbol. You can draw it on your body or onto objects you wish to protect. You can create charms with it, etch it into a candle and then burn that candle to bring you protection, sew it onto your bag to protect your possessions, or trace it over your front door to protect your property, for example. The only limit here is your imagination, so get creative and see what you come up with.

Essential Oils

Certain scents are associated with protection as well. A great way to incorporate these is by using essential oils. You can dab them on your wrists or your third eye chakra to help bring protection.

Please note, you must never apply essential oils directly to your skin; please make sure you use a suitable carrier oil, such as olive oil, coconut oil, or jojoba oil. The International Federation of Aromatherapists notes that cosmetic product safety assessors will only approve those which are comprised of 1 percent essential oils, and the Aromatherapy Trade Council recommends five drops of oil per 10 mL of carrier oil, or three drops if you have sensitive skin (and I would always err on the side of caution).[6]

You could also create your own oil by adding dried herbs of your choosing in a suitable base oil, such as virgin olive oil, and leaving it to settle for two to four weeks. Some good scents and herbs for protection include clove, garlic, bay leaves, star anise, sandalwood, and pine needles.

6. "Legislation Affecting Aromatherapists and Product Designers," International Federation of Aromatherapists, accessed March 31, 2025, https://ifaroma.org/en_GB/home/registrants/aromatherapy-legislation; "How to Use Essential Oils," Aromatherapy Trade Council, accessed March 31, 2025, https://www.a-t-c.org.uk/about-aromatherapy/how-to-use-essential-oils/.

You may wish to make up an incantation to say as you anoint yourself with the oil, such as "I am protected—no harm will befall me."

Protective Sachet

A sachet is a small pouch that you fill with items and objects that represent your intention—in this case, protection—and then carry with you. You can add whatever you want to your sachet so long as it isn't too heavy and is safe to carry on your person. You may wish to include the herbs mentioned previously, drawings of protective symbols, or crystals. At the end of this chapter, I will provide a small table of herbs, crystals, and such that have protective qualities, which you can use for inspiration as to what to include in your sachet.

As you fill your sachet, focus on your intent (protection). You may wish to state your intention as you build your sachet to further empower it or chant the word *protection* as you do so.

Crystal Protections

Wearing or holding crystals with protective qualities is another simple way of protecting yourself. Check the table at the end of this section to find out which crystals are generally associated with protection.

Invoking Guides

You can invoke your guides to protect you as and when needed. This involves specifically calling on them and asking them to protect you. Your guide may be an animal spirit, an ancestor, or some other being. There are many meditations, rituals, and other exercises out there to help you find your guide, so if working with guides is not something you are familiar with then use some of the fantastic resources out there to see if it may benefit you. I personally work a lot with animal guides, and if that is an area that interests you, then check out the protection table where I list several animals associated with protection.

Invoking Angels

For those who work with angels, you can call on angelic energies to protect you as and when needed. The Archangel Michael is especially good to call, as he is known as "the protector of mankind." Whilst there are many prayers associated with him, one of the most well-known is the Catholic "Prayer to Saint Michael the Archangel." There are several variations and translations of this prayer, but it often resembles this one:

> Saint Michael the Archangel, defend us in battle; be our protection against the wickedness and snares of the devil. May God rebuke him, we humbly pray: and do thou, O Prince of the heavenly host, by the power of God, cast into hell Satan and all the evil spirits who prowl about the world seeking the ruin of souls. Amen.[7]

Veiling

Veiling is a practice that has become more popular with younger practitioners in recent years. Simply put, it is the act of wearing a scarf, a veil, or similar so that it covers your crown chakra and creates a physical barrier that can protect your energy. I personally find scarves and such items uncomfortable to wear, so it is not a practice I engage with, but considering its growing popularity I thought it was worth mentioning here.

Protection Correspondences

This list of correspondences highlights ones that are generally associated with protection. You can use these or other symbols that you may be familiar with. These can be incorporated into the methods we discussed in this section; for example, if you want to practice veiling, you may choose a dark blue veil. If you wish to create a sachet, you may want to include a bloodstone crystal, some pinches of lavender and rue, and a murex shell.

Animals: Alligators, bears, cats, coral, crabs (emotional protection), dogs, lions, owls, sharks, tigers, wolves

7. Andrew Hofer and Jonah Teller, *Nine Days with Saint Michael* (Magnificat, 2021).

Colours: Black, dark blue

Crystals: Aquamarine, bloodstone, fluorite, garnet, hematite, jade, black jasper, lapis lazuli, obsidian, onyx, smoky quartz, tiger's eye

Herbs/Plants/Trees: Chives, cinnamon, cinquefoil, cloves, dill, dragon's blood, fennel seeds, frankincense, garlic, heather, heliotrope, hickory, juniper, lavender, mandrake, marshmallow root, mistletoe, rue, thistle, thyme, parsley, peony, sandalwood, St. John's wort, vervain

Symbols: The Christian cross, the equal-armed cross, eye of Horus, Hamsa hand, iron nails

Other Objects: Auger shell, holy water, the murex shell, salt

Cleansing

We have focused on how to protect yourself against negative energy, but sometimes it is unavoidable. Situations where the negativity is too strong or where we are exposed to this negativity for a prolonged period can break through even the best of shields and protective measures. In these situations, we need to know how best to cleanse ourselves of that negative energy.

The act of cleansing is great to perform regularly, as often we can be exposed to negativity without realising it (including both negativity from others and our own negative mindsets). You may also find that different methods of cleansing work better depending on exactly what you are cleansing yourself of. For example, I find that if the negative energy is manifesting from my own mindset, then a ritual bath works better for me in dispelling this energy. If I find myself feeling heavy and anxious as a result of negative energy buildup, then a sound bath is my preferred way of cleansing myself of this energy. If I am looking for a more general, light approach, then the smoke cleanse is my go-to method. As with all of the exercises in this book, half of the fun of energy work is trying these different techniques and discovering which works best for you.

Showering

Water is a great cleanser, and taking a shower is a simple cleansing method that can easily be built into your day-to-day routine. You can keep it simple by visualising the water washing away any negativity as you shower, or you can add some soaps, oils, or body scrubs that include oils, herbs, and such that are associated with cleansing. Great ones to incorporate include anything with lavender, rosemary, vanilla, rose, and lemon.

Ritual Bath

Ritual baths are one of my favourite ritual types, especially for cleansing. Ritual bathing has a rich history and has been practised by many different cultures for hundreds of years. You can add herbs and oils to your bath (the recommendation from the Aromatherapy Trade Council is four to six drops of essential oil in a bath[8]), sea salt, even place crystals around your bath (some crystals are not compatible with water, so it is best to keep them around the bath rather than placing them directly in the water).

Add your ingredients to your bath as the water is running and mix them in a clockwise direction. As you bathe, focus on the herbs and the water soaking up any negativity you may have picked up, releasing all that may be holding you back, and instead opening yourself up to the positive energies that surround you.

White Light Visualisation

Cleansing can be performed using visualisation, essentially by connecting with universal energy and using this to cleanse our energy. Visualise a ball of white light floating above you; this universal energy is pure and healing. See it like a waterfall, as this energy flows down through your body. This light picks up any negative energy you may be harbouring as it washes through you, out through your feet, and into the earth.

8. "How to use Essential Oils," Aromatherapy Trade Council, accessed March 31, 2025, https://www.a-t-c.org.uk/about-aromatherapy/how-to-use-essential-oils/.

Sound Vibration

Sound waves are energy, and the vibration of this energy can be used to cleanse and heal. Singing bowls, especially crystal singing bowls, and gongs are great to create the right vibrations to achieve this. If you can get to a live sound bath session, then great! Otherwise, there are some wonderful videos online you can lie back and listen to as you focus on any negative energies being removed from your body. I will go into a bit more detail about the relationship between sound and energy later in the book, but for a "deep cleanse" I highly recommend a crystal singing bowl or gong session.

Smoke Cleanse

A smoke cleanse is best performed with incense. Any smoke will do, but the smoke of an incense stick tends to smell nicer than that of a bonfire! If you can find one that is of a scent associated with cleansing, then it will pack an extra punch; again, rose, lavender, rosemary, and lemon are all associated with cleansing, as is sandalwood and frankincense. You can also use bundles of dried herbs if you prefer, although these do tend to give off more smoke, which can be irritating to some.

Light your incense or herbs and position it so the smoke is directed toward you. Use your hands to waft the smoke over you, from your head to your toes. Visualise the smoke carrying away any negative energies. As I do so, I tend to chant "I cleanse myself of all negativity, in this world and in the astral" to aid my intent.

Egg Cleanse

Egg cleanses have grown in popularity in recent years. They have a rich history and have been used in many different cultures. There are two parts to an egg cleanse: the cleansing itself and then interpreting the cleanse by breaking the egg into water.

Performing an Egg Cleanse

For the cleansing, take an egg and, starting at the crown of your head, slowly move it down your body from your head to your toes.

Be sure to get each side of the body, including your arms and legs. Visualise the egg drawing the negativity from your body as you do so, including mental, emotional, physical, or spiritual.

We can then use the egg to help determine where this negativity has come from or what form it has been picked up in, which can help us pinpoint sources of negativity so we may avoid them in the future. This is the interpretation part of the egg cleanse.

Once you have finished drawing out the negativity with the egg, take a bowl or a glass of water and crack the egg open into it. You can then use the shapes and patterns it forms in the water to give you the relevant information.

If the egg sinks to the bottom of the glass or bowl, this is a sign that the cleanse was successful, and all negativity has been removed. If even part of the egg floats, this signifies that there is still negativity present and that further work is needed to uproot and remove it.

If there is any discoloration to the egg, such as the yolk being grey or cloudy, then this is seen as a sign that someone is wishing ill upon you. Small bubbles present in the water indicate that negativity has been removed, but larger balloon-like bubbles suggest that there is a situation you are stuck in that you are struggling to escape.

If the egg forms into webs, this can be a sign that there is a situation or a circumstance you feel trapped in, or that there are others out there who are jealous of you and are wanting you to fail. Spikes or needles formed by the egg can represent the energy that was removed.

I have to admit, I am a bit of a sceptic when it comes to the interpretation of the cleanse, but I know others who swear by it. I personally find the cleanse itself extremely effective and will often perform the interpretation anyway, as the results can lead to some interesting introspection.

Chapter Three Reflections

Being able to protect and cleanse your energy are extremely useful skills. Honestly, if you get to the end of this book and decide that energy healing is not for you, I still recommend that you learn a couple of basic protection and cleansing techniques. Even if it is just used as a psychological exercise, they can really aid us in managing the difficulties and challenges we may face in our day-to-day lives. Below are some questions and exercises to help you get a grip on what we have learned in this chapter.

1. Over the course of the next few days, try three of the protection exercises. Which three did you choose? How easy or difficult did you find them? Do you feel it made a difference as to how you felt by the end of the day compared to how you usually feel?
2. Over the course of the next few days, try three of the cleansing exercises. Which three did you choose? How did you feel after compared to how you felt before? Were there any sensations that arose as you were performing them? Which one felt the most effective, and why do you think that is?
3. Think about the exercise in chapter 1 where you listed out the sources of negative energy you may come across in your day-to-day life. Which of the protection methods do you think would best aid you in those situations and why?

CHAPTER FOUR
Energy Healing

At this stage, you should have an understanding of the basics of energy work. Throughout this chapter, you should be able to see why that is so important and how the concepts we have explored relate to energy healing. From being aware of the ethical considerations of such work to being able to sense the energy you will use to heal and be healed to being able to cleanse and protect yourself from negative energies, it is all a necessary foundation to systems of energy healing.

This is by far the largest chapter in the book. Trying to structure it so it doesn't feel as though I am just throwing a lot of information out there that could be overwhelming was difficult! Especially because there are so many different energy healing systems out there. As we noted in the introduction, the majority of these come from the East and from cultures that have been well versed in these practices for hundreds of years. Over the decades, many of these have made their way into Western practices and, in a lot of cases, were amended to suit a more Western audience. It is necessary to remember though that for many, these systems are more than just energy healing systems; they are intrinsically tied into their beliefs, their culture, and their way of life.

It is important to have an understanding of such and practise any method with the utmost respect for those whose culture it is a part of. Where possible, seek to learn from those whose culture these systems are from. I am of a Western background, and having spent a couple of years tracing back my family tree, I can honestly say I'm about as English as they get. I do not pretend to be an expert in any one method, and I am conscious that I do not have the cultural experiences to be able to guide you toward a much deeper understanding in many of these areas. Instead, I aim to introduce you to these methods and the techniques of energy healing at a practical "top level" view. The hope is that you will find one that resonates with you, which you will go on to explore and deepen your knowledge of. When you do, I highly recommend seeking out those with the cultural experience of the techniques you are interested in. I can say from having worked and studied under such people myself, it is truly a blessing to be allowed to learn directly from those with such understanding.

One thing to note is that there are a lot of systems out there that others have devised. For example, the Emotion Code was devised by Dr. Bradley Nelson, DC, and states that our emotional baggage is the underlying cause of our illnesses and negativity.[9] The Emotion Code has been designed as a system to help you identify these negative emotional responses and where in the body they sit so you can start to heal them. I use this as an example only because it seems to have become quite popular with other energy practitioners I work with, but it is not one I have personally worked with myself. As such, I won't go into any detail about any of these sorts of systems; I will only be talking about those I have personally experienced and are more widely known, accepted, and practised.

Many of these individual's systems have very good reviews and are rated very highly by others in the community (including the Emotion Code), so I urge you to do your research and see if there are any others out there that resonate with you. Just because I have not written about them does not mean that I am actively wanting to dissuade you from trying such approaches. Just remember the guidance from chapter 1 regarding the dangers to look out for to ensure that any sources you use are legitimate.

You can use these techniques to heal your own energy and to heal others. If you do intend on healing others, then I highly recommend that you become proficient with the exercises in chapter 2 and spend time practising them on yourself. If you aren't confident in these basics before you go on

9. Bradley Nelson, *The Emotion Code: How to Release Your Trapped Emotions for Abundant Health, Love, and Happiness* (Vermillion, 2019).

to practise energy healing on another, there is a real possibility that you could not only harm yourself but also your client.

We will start by looking at the preparations you need to make for energy healing, both for healing yourself and healing others. We will then kick off our journey into energy healing techniques themselves, starting with colour healing. I know that colour healing may sound simplistic, or even out of place, but understanding the energy of colours and using these in healing is extremely effective. Not only is it simple yet powerful, but when we start to look at techniques such as chakras and auras, you will see that colour plays a large part in these therapies too. As such, colour healing felt like the perfect choice to lead us into the wider world of energy healing.

From there, we will look at meridians. This isn't an energy healing technique per se, but rather a system as to how energy works in the body. Understanding this will further the foundations we have built to move on to other systems of energy healing.

Then we will move on to looking at some well-established practices such as Qi Gong, chakras, and auras. Finally, we will look at other forms of energy healing that aren't necessarily "systems" as such but are very beneficial in aiding us in healing—this includes using sound, crystals, and tree energy, amongst others.

I will admit, it was difficult to know how to order this chapter. I thought about doing an "A to Z," but with some of these systems being somewhat related, that didn't work. So, whilst this chapter may feel as though I've just thrown a whole load of information on a page, I promise there is a logic to it that should hopefully become apparent as you make your way through this chapter.

Preparing for Healing

Whether you are practising energy healing on yourself or on another (and I will talk more on the specifics of using healing on another later in this section), there are certain steps you will need to take to prepare yourself.

These will be relevant no matter which method of energy healing you choose.

Now, I will admit, I am not the sort who engages in elaborate rituals or who will dedicate an entire afternoon to cleansing my space. Why overcomplicate things when often the simplest of approaches can be the most effective? The steps I outline below are the bare minimum, so please do not skip them. Working with energy can have a profound effect, yet also serious consequences if not done properly.

Your Physical Space

First, consider your physical space. There is a whole section later in this book about working with your environment (your home, your office, etc.), and how to best optimise the energy in these spaces, but for now we don't need to focus on that level of detail. We want to ensure our space is safe and positive to elicit the best results, a space that you will be comfortable in and won't be disturbed. Somewhere you (or another) can sit or lie comfortably without fear of interruption for the duration of the healing is a must. I personally find that dim lighting helps my mind settle, and some meditation music quietly in the background helps me get into the right mindset for healing.

Cleansing

Ensure that you have used one of the methods listed in the section on cleansing to make sure that you have cleansed your own energy as best as possible before using healing. This is especially important when performing healing on others.

Protection

As with the cleansing, make sure that you have used one of the methods listed in the section on protection to ensure you have adequate safety measures in place. Again, this is especially important when performing healing on others, as it is not just your own energy you will be interacting with.

Connecting with the Energy

Make sure that you take a moment to find your power centre and connect with your own energy before connecting with the healing energies you will be using. Remember, you do not use your own energy for healing, and so you can use exercises such as the roots meditation and the breathing exercises in the previous chapters to connect with the universal energy and act as a conduit for this healing energy to flow through. Some systems, such as emotional freedom technique (EFT), are focused on using techniques that will improve your energy flow which will bring healing, whilst others, such as reiki, focus on connecting with universal energy and using this for healing.

Body Scanning

This technique can be used on yourself or on that which you are planning on performing healing on. Body scanning allows us to "check in" and gain a top-level understanding as to where there may be blockages in the energy or if there are any particular areas we should focus on.

Performing a Body Scan

Sit somewhere you won't be disturbed and clear your mind. Feel the energy in the palm of your hands; you could perform the energy orb exercise, connect with your power centre and see that energy flow into your palms, or perform any other method you may have tried so far to help you connect to energy.

When you are ready, lift your hands to the top of your head and slowly bring them down in front of your body (or the body of the person you are healing), right down as far as you wish (I personally just scan the seven main chakras), and back up if you want. I like to think of it as being at an airport with someone who has a manual security scanning wand, passing it up and down my body. As you do, feel the energy you have collected in your palms acting as the reader, skimming over your (or your client's) energy, and "going off" at any areas that don't feel right.

How will you know where there is a blockage? To me, it is a physical feeling; the energy feels different to the rest of the energy; it can feel heavier, slower, or I may get a sinking feeling in the pit of my stomach. For others, it may be other physical sensations such as your hairs standing on edge or maybe you hear a "beeping" sound—very much like an airport scanner! As with all things in energy work, it is worth practising this exercise on yourself before you attempt to try it on others to gain an understanding as to how blockages and such feel to you.

• • •

Remember, these steps in preparing for energy healing are the bare minimum. There may be other preparations you wish to work into your practice that help you, such as saying a specific mantra or prayer or burning a certain incense. As always, discover what works best for you and roll with it.

Now that we have undergone our preparations, let's take a look at the different energy healing concepts and techniques and how best to use them in your own practice, beginning with colour healing.

Working with Energy Through Colour

Intangible concepts can also have an energy all their own. Science has proven that colours can change our mood and our emotions. Many energy healing practitioners believe that each colour has a different vibration that can influence the vibration of our own energy. It is one of the reasons that many of the exercises in this book involve visualising bubbles of light.

Each colour has its own associations, and these tend to be very similar across most cultures. Where these have come from is difficult to know. One theory that I personally find very interesting, especially in the context of energy work, is that of Jung's theory of collective consciousness.

Carl Jung was a student of Sigmund Freud. Whilst Freud came up with the theory of the "Id," our ego, Jung expanded on this and added another element that affects our development. This is the collective consciousness, the belief that our subconscious is not just a repository of our own personal experiences but also of those of all of humanity. Every person on the planet shares in this collective consciousness. We carry these memories of our ancestors in this consciousness and use them to bring structure into the world. For me, personally, this is similar to when people talk about the Akashic records (a vast library that contains all the knowledge of our human experience). This could explain why we as a species seem to have applied very similar concepts across different time periods and civilizations, including the meanings of colours. The sum of this collective consciousness, this human experience and the energy created by this belief, is an energy we can then connect with and use in our own workings.

Rather than this being some abstract collective consciousness, it could be years of tangible psychological programming; think of how long the colour pink has been used to symbolise love. Most of us have grown up learning that the colour pink has been associated with love, but how many of us can pinpoint exactly when or how we were taught this?

This is the reason that I personally believe the energy of colour is so effective, but this is just my view on it; you may have a completely different opinion. No matter the how, for many colour is a simple yet effective way of connecting to energy and using it to strengthen our own energetic selves.

Colours are also strongly associated with the chakras and the aura. The different shades of these specific colours can give us an insight as to where we may need to focus our energies to help us heal and improve our state of being. This is just another example as to how colour influences energy work and why it is important to have a basic understanding of it.

Whilst there are generally accepted associations of each colour, different people may have different associations. These can often be based on personal experience. White is the colour most often associated with purity and innocence, and black is often associated with grief. However, if I had lost a close loved one and at their funeral was a centrepiece of white flowers, I might actually associate the colour white with grief, at least for a time.

Colour Association Exercise

In this exercise I have listed some basic common colours. Think about what emotions, thoughts, feelings, or images immediately come to mind when you read them. Make a note of these in your journal. Take some time to reflect if there are any particular reasons you have the associations you do. Not only will it help you understand how you can best interact with colour energy specifically, but it will also give you an interesting insight as to how you generally interact with energy. I'll provide mine after this, so don't read on until you have done this exercise, as I wouldn't want your answers influenced by mine!

White:
Pink:
Yellow:
Black:
Green:
Orange:
Red:
Blue:
Gold:
Brown:
Silver:
Purple:

Below are the associations I came up with when I consider the list. As you will see, mine are a mixture of feelings and images, and again this is based on my own personal experience. I spent several years working on a lavender farm, so whenever I hear the word "purple," I always get a picture of lavender in my mind, and I can smell the scent as if I were back in the fields.

White: Innocence, purity, the goddess Athena, blank slate and new beginnings, cleansing

Pink: Love, comfort, self-love, roses, hugs, stuffed animals

Yellow: Bees, happiness, citrine
Black: Death, curses, emptiness, meditation, depth
Green*:* Healing, grass, money
Orange: Happiness, socialness, abundance
Red: Passion, desire, loyalty
Blue: Peace, the sea, sadness
Gold: Masculine energies, strength, success, abundance, leadership, the sun
Brown: Murkiness, hard work, dedication
Silver: Feminine energies, the moon, jewellery, luxury, beauty
Purple: Lavender, spirituality, royalty, psychic abilities and intuition, peace

So how do we use these energies in healing? Let's say for example you are going through a breakup and are feeling rejected. Looking at the list you have written, what colours could help you come to terms with this and heal? From my list, I could use white to help cleanse me of negative energies and see this as a new beginning. I could use pink for comfort and self-love, or purple to help me find peace. I would probably want to avoid the colour blue, as I associate blue with sadness.

• • •

There are many ways you can connect with these energies and easily incorporate them into your daily life to help bring their healing energy to you. You may have also written down some images or physical representations in your description. For example, I've listed "stuffed toy" for pink, as I know I associated pink with comfort, and my childhood stuffed toys still bring me comfort (even though I'm closer to forty than I would like, I'm not ashamed to admit it!). So, I could grab one of my stuffed animals for comfort. You could wear an item of that colour or a piece of jewellery, such as a bracelet, that radiates that particular colour. You could also burn a candle of that colour and use this to connect with the energy, or you can simply meditate on that colour.

One exercise I personally find quite useful in this respect is the energy shielding exercise, but I will instead see that energy bubble as whatever colour I want to work with. I visualise this bubble of colour wrapping itself around me, embracing my own energy with its healing.

You could also try drawing or painting a picture using primarily that colour and different shades of it. Another option is to invest in a colour-changing light and select the colour of your choice. I'm sure there are many other ways you can incorporate colour energy into your life that I have not thought of, so get creative!

The power that colours have to influence our energy is incredibly simple and easy to incorporate into everyday rituals. Whether you are a beginner to energy work or even a seasoned practitioner, don't underestimate the power of colour in energy healing.

Meridians

Meridians can be described as the energetic pathways within our body, allowing energy to flow through us in the same way our veins and arteries allow our blood to flow through our bodies. The meridian system comes from ancient Chinese tradition and is still in use today. Whilst it is not a healing system per se, it forms the basis of several types of energy healing methods, so I wanted to provide a brief overview.

This network is split into two categories: the Jingmai, which are the meridian channels themselves, and the Luomai, which are the associated vessels or collaterals. Think of the Jingma as the energy points and the Luomai as the veins and arteries that connect these points.

The main meridians that we tend to work with are the twelve principal meridians and the eight extraordinary meridians. Each of the twelve principal meridians are associated with an organ or area of the body:

1. The Lung Channel of Hand Taiyin (LU) is associated with our lungs. This pathway starts at the front of the shoulder and runs down the outer side of the arm, ending at the thumb.

2. The Heart Channel of Hand Shaoyin (HT) is associated with the heart. This pathway runs from the little finger, along the inside of the arm, and up to the armpit.
3. The Pericardium Channel of Hand Jueyin (PC) is associated with the pericardium. The pericardium is an Eastern concept rather than a physical organ and is the "heart defence." It is also associated with the heart. It runs from the tip of the middle finger, along the middle of the arm, and finishes in the chest area just below the armpit.
4. The Sanjiao Channel of Hand Shaoyang (also known as the Triple Warmer) (TB) is associated with the triple burner. Again, this triple burner is more of a concept than a physical organ; the upper burner is associated with the organs in the thorax that are used for breathing, the middle burner is associated with the organs at the top of the stomach and digestive processes, whilst the lower burner is associated with the organs beneath the stomach. If the triple burner is flowing strong, then all our organs will work together in harmony. It runs from the tips of the ring finger, up the arm, over the shoulder and the back of the neck, before passing in front of the ear and then channelling across to end at the point of the eyebrow closest to your ear.
5. The Small Intestine Channel of Hand Taiyang (SI) is associated with the small intestine. This pathway runs from the tip of the little finger, up the arm, up across the shoulder blade, up the side of the neck and across the cheek, ending just in front of the ear.
6. The Large Intestine Channel of Hand Yangming (also known as the colon meridian) (LI) is associated with the large intestine. It runs from the tip of the index finger, up the arm, across the shoulder blade, up the side of the neck, across the cheek, and ends just below the nose.
7. The Spleen Channel of Foot Taiyin (SP) is associated with the spleen. This pathway runs from the big toe, up the inside of the

leg, up across the stomach and the side of the chest, and ends below the shoulder.

8. The Kidney Channel of Foot Shaoyin (KI) is associated with the kidneys. This pathway runs from the sole of the foot, along the inside of the leg, through the centre of the torso, and ends just below the collarbone.
9. The Liver Channel of Foot Jueyin (LV or LI) is associated with the liver. It runs from the big toe, up the inside of the leg, up the front side of the body, and ends just below the nipple.
10. The Gallbladder Channel of Foot Shaoyang (GB) is associated with the gallbladder. This pathway runs from the outer corner of the eye, up over the side of the face and the forehead, down the head, and then down the side of the body before ending at the fourth toe.
11. The Bladder Channel of Foot Taiyang (BL or UB) is associated with the urinary bladder. It starts at the inside corner of the eye and runs up the forehead, down the back of the head, down the back and the back of the leg, before ending at the little toe.
12. The Stomach Channel of Foot Yangming (ST) is associated with the stomach. It starts beneath the eye and down to the mouth, before heading back up the forehead. From here, it runs back down and through the throat and the torso, then down the front of the leg and ends at the second toe.

The eight extraordinary meridians are primarily associated with our energetic being and help our life-force energy flow throughout the body. They don't have any points in the body of their own exactly but instead borrow from the twelve principal meridians. Think of them more as storage vessels for energy, directing energy where it needs to go and connecting the other twelve meridians.

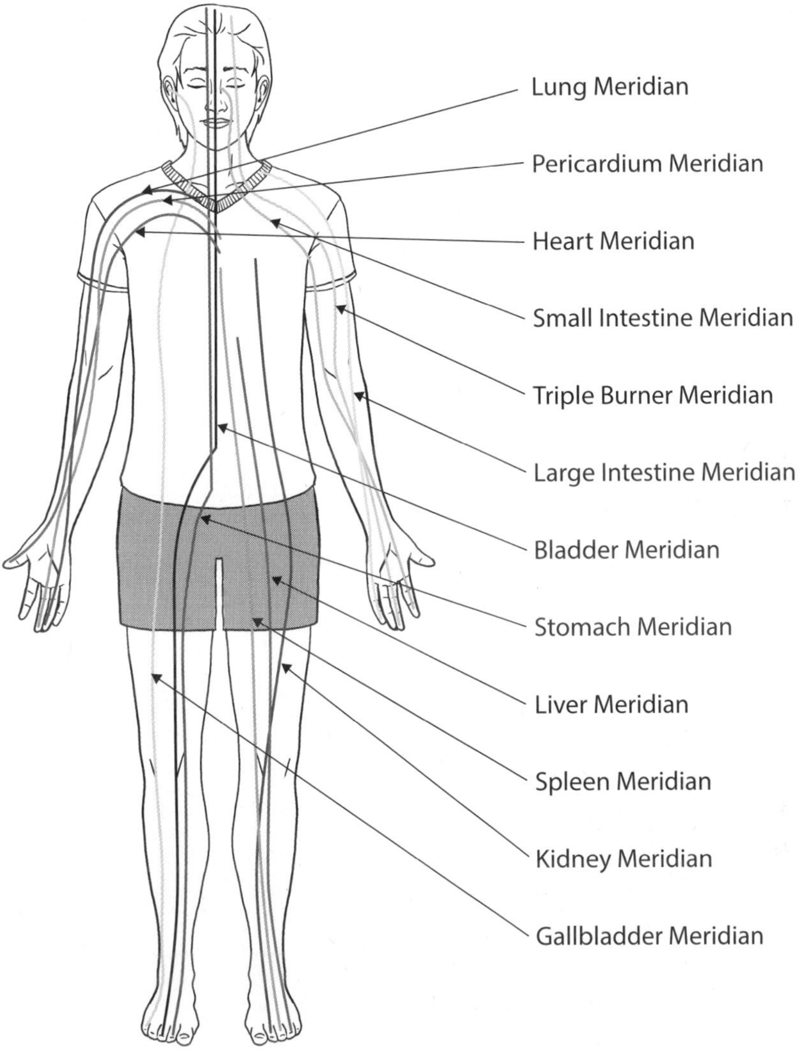

Lung Meridian
Pericardium Meridian
Heart Meridian
Small Intestine Meridian
Triple Burner Meridian
Large Intestine Meridian
Bladder Meridian
Stomach Meridian
Liver Meridian
Spleen Meridian
Kidney Meridian
Gallbladder Meridian

Figure 1: The 12 Principal Meridians

1. The Conception Vessel (Ren Mai) represents conception and birth, whether this is physically (the birth of a child) or new ideas. It is associated with our feminine energy and governs self-love, nurturing, and intimate relationships.
2. The Governing Vessel (Du Mai) represents endurance, independence, and grounding. It can help us find our motivation and put ourselves out into the world to achieve our dreams.
3. The Penetrating Vessel (Chong Mai) can be used to help people break free of negative habits and trauma. It also helps us answer those big life questions, such as who we are and what our purpose in the world is.
4. The Girdle Vessel (Dai Mai) is associated with peace and the clarity of mind needed for decision-making.
5. The Yin Linking Vessel (Yin Wei Mai) represents compassion. It can help us love ourselves and deal with emotional pain. It allows us to walk our path with love and happiness in our hearts.
6. The Yang Linking Vessel (Yang Wei Mai) can help release old patterns and habits, which can allow us to move forward and grow.
7. The Yin Heel Vessel (Yin Qiao Mai) is associated with our self-worth and can help us define our values and feel confident in living them.
8. The Yang Heel Vessel (Yang Qiao Mai) is associated with movement and can help us better live in the present moment.

These meridians are used in therapies such as acupuncture, where thin needles are placed in the skin at specific points along the meridians to help balance our energy flow. If acupuncture doesn't sound like your kind of thing (I have to admit, it isn't mine), then you could instead try EFT tapping. EFT stands for "emotional freedom technique," and instead of needles you use your fingertips to tap on the areas of the body where these meridians lie to help you heal. You could use specific crystals or oils that suit the association of the meridian and place them on the location of the meridian to stimulate the energy or connect to universal energy and see this energy being channelled through your body to the specific meridian and see if this has any impact on your own energetic self.

There are also other practices, such as Qi Gong, which use certain poses to help stimulate certain meridians, which we will take a look at next.

Qi Gong

Qi Gong originated in ancient China, with the first known documentation of it dating from roughly 2,000 years ago. It is a fundamental component of traditional Chinese medicine, and is also practised as a martial art. There are many different forms of Qi Gong, so rather than go into the specifics, I will instead just provide an overview of Qi Gong as a whole.

Qi means "breath, or vital energy," whilst *Gong* translates as "gathering." So, Qi Gong essentially means the gathering of Qi (energy), and we harness this energy to bring balance to our being. It uses breath, movement, and meditation to help us improve our energy flow and bring balance to the body. I personally find that I really physically feel the energy when I'm performing Qi Gong; I can feel it in my hands and direct it through and around my body. In fact, I know of others who really struggle with visualising energy but absolutely love Qi Gong because it allows them to feel it in a way that other practices don't.

Qi Gong movements were originally based on animals and the movements they make, and one of the earliest forms of Qi Gong is the "Five Animal Frolics," which farmers and those who worked in the fields would perform at the end of the workday to help release tension in their bodies. Qi Gong expanded and became integrated with the meridians.

As a type of moving meditation, this practice helps remove blockages so that our energy—our Qi—can move freely throughout our bodies, or our meridians. It focuses on gentle, flowing movements that follow our breath to guide the Qi around our bodies. Because of this, it is not just our energetic body that it has a positive impact upon but our physical body also.

I personally find that Qi Gong really resonates with me. I will try and find some time to perform a short routine to help me better connect with my own energy and encourage a healthy flow throughout my body. I find this an especially good starting point if I am feeling a bit off or have been struggling to connect with energy in general.

If you wish to try Qi Gong, then I recommend finding a teacher and attending a couple of lessons, at least until you have the moves mastered. There are videos online you can watch, but some of the moves can appear complicated at first, so I recommend finding someone to teach you. However, below are some movements you can try out to help you understand if Qi Gong may be for you.

Remember, there are many different types of Qi Gong, and whilst some have similar moves, they may be called something completely different depending on the style you are practising. So, if you see a movement I have listed here under a different name, don't fret.

Knocking on the Door of Life (Also Known as the Spinning Drum)

Always start by finding your posture. You want your feet roughly hip width apart, knees slightly bent, and arms loose by your side. Clear your mind and focus on your breathing; remember, the movements follow our breath, so keeping a steady breath is very important.

This is often used as a warmup or opening exercise. With your arms loose, rotate from the waist and swing your arms around, one to the back and lightly tapping your lower back, and the other to the front and lightly tapping your hip area, and then swing them the other way. Repeat this swinging motion, but this time tap the shoulders and the back. Perform this as many times as you wish. This is good for getting the Qi moving.

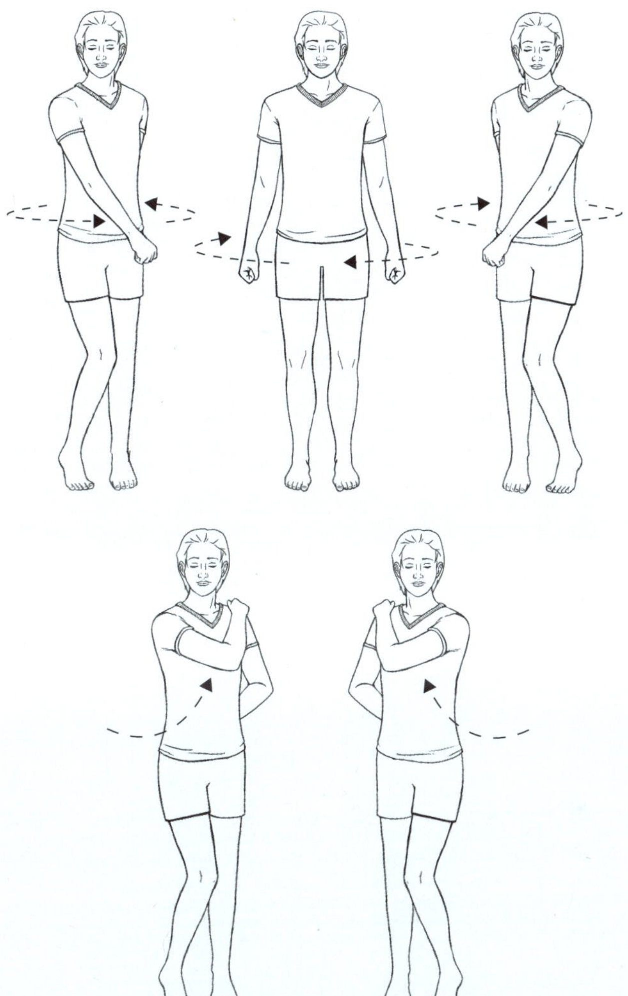

Figure 2: Knocking on the Door of Life

Pulling Down the Heavens

Lift your arms from your side, palms facing up, out, and toward the sky, inhaling as you do so. Once your arms are above your head, turn your palms to face the ground and bring your hands down with your elbows out and hands travelling down past the front of your face and your body as you exhale. Then repeat.

Figure 3: Pulling Down the Heavens

Pushing the Wave

Stand with one foot forward, knees soft. Bring your hands to your hips and, as you exhale, push them in front of you—as if you were pushing a wave out to sea. Inhale and bring your hands back in toward your hips. Repeat.

Figure 4: Pushing the Wave

EFT Tapping

Emotional freedom technique (EFT) tapping is a method through which we focus on what is blocking us and then tap our fingers on specific meridians to release that energy. EFT is a system devised by Gary Craig in the 1990s based on the teachings of Dr. Roger Callahan's Thought Field Therapy. It has become a very popular method. In fact, my first introduction to it was at a Buddhist festival many years back. This can be used on yourself, or you can treat a client using this method.

There are several specific meridians used in EFT tapping, mostly focused around the head area. These are:

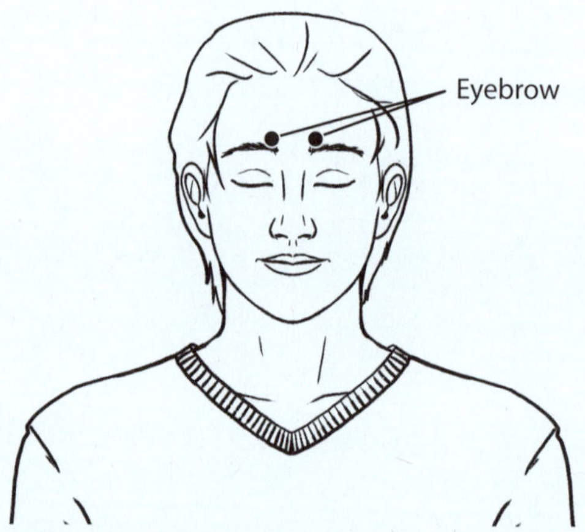

Figure 5: Eyebrow Point (EB) EFT Tapping

Eyebrow Point (EB)

Located at the beginning of each eyebrow, close to the bridge of the nose (this is two points). It is associated with the bladder meridian, and it can aid us in releasing hurt and sadness and healing emotionally.

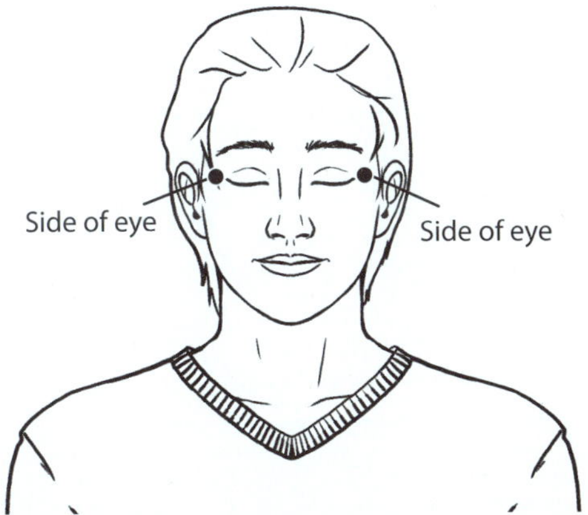

Figure 6: Side of the Eye (ES) EFT Tapping

Side of the Eye (ES)

This point is on the bone alongside the outside of each eye, and it is associated with the gallbladder. A blockage here can lead us to harbouring and holding on to resentment and anger, and clearing this meridian can encourage compassion and clarity.

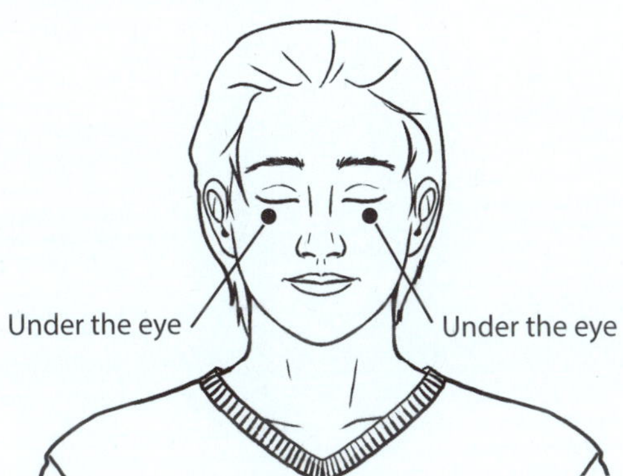

Figure 7: Under the Eye (UE) EFT Tapping

Under the Eye (UE)

This point is on the bone directly under each eye, around the centre of the bottom of the eye/close to the nose. It is associated with the stomach meridian. An imbalance here can cause feelings of nervousness and a lack of acceptance, where instead we should be feeling peace and contentment.

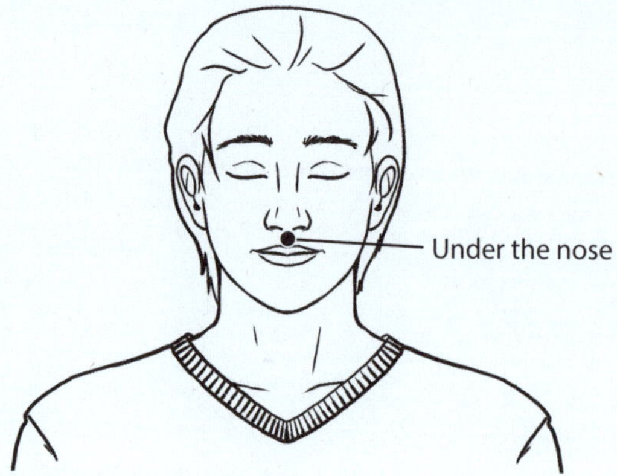

Figure 8: Under the Nose (UN) EFT Tapping

Under the Nose (UN)

Located directly under the nose and above the upper lip, this point is associated with the governing vessel. Working with this point allows us to release shame and helps us feel empowered and accepting of ourselves.

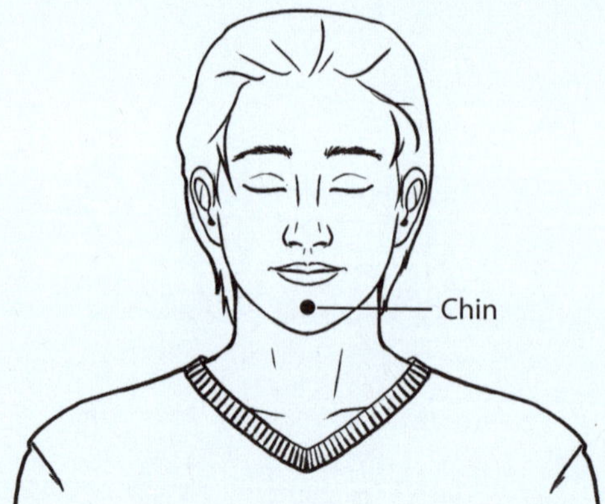

Figure 9: Chin Point (CP) EFT Tapping

Chin Point (CP)

Located in the crease just below the bottom lip and above the chin, this point is associated with the central meridian and can help us overcome confusion, find clarity, and establish confidence in ourselves.

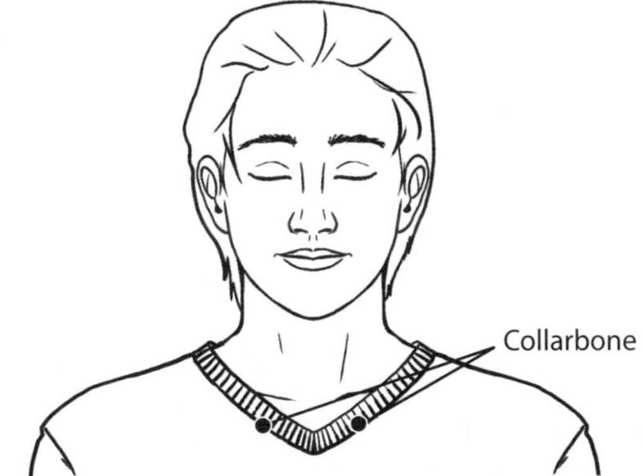

Figure 10: Collarbone Point (CB) EFT Tapping

Collar Bone Point (CB)

This is two points. Find where your collar bones meet in the centre, and then bring your finger down an inch, and then out an inch each way to find each of the points. These points are associated with the kidneys and can help us in moving forward confidently. It again promotes clarity and confidence.

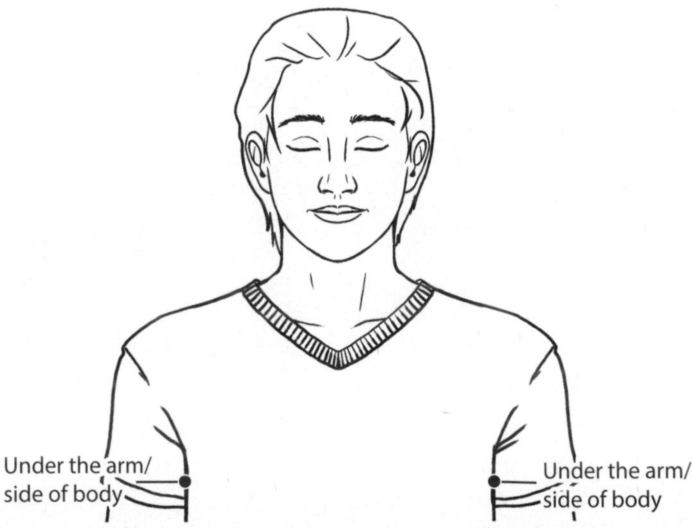

Figure 11: Underarm Point (UA) EFT Tapping

Underarm Point (UA)

On either side of your body, roughly four inches below the armpit. This point is associated with the spleen meridian and can help us release guilt, worry, and obsessive feelings.

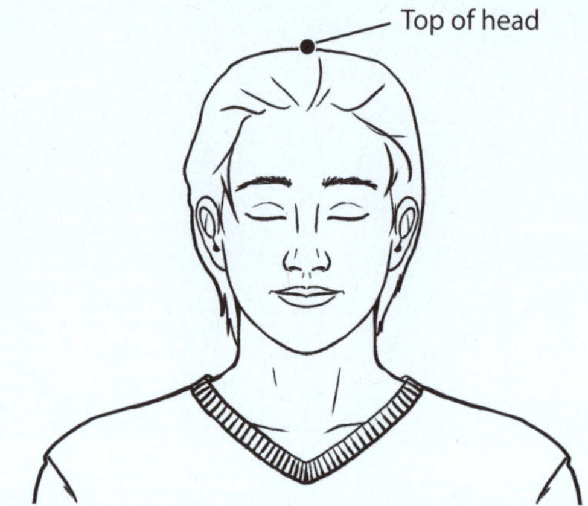

Figure 12: Top of the Head Point (TH) EFT Tapping

Top of the Head Point (TH)

Located directly at the crown of your head. It is associated with our governing vessel, which is connected to many other meridians and encourages an open, spiritual connection and inner balance.

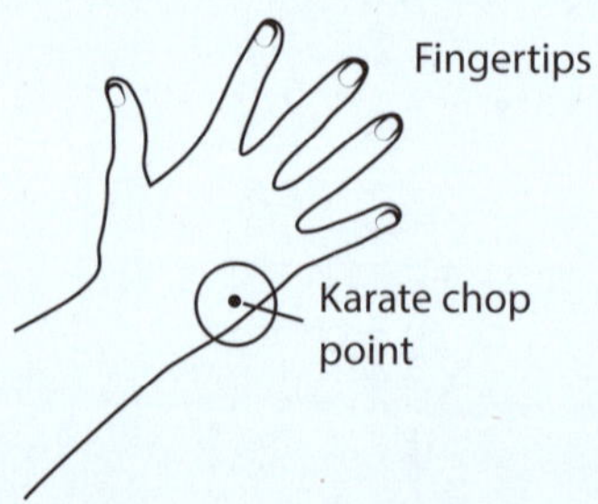

Figure 13: The Karate Chop Point EFT Tapping

The Karate Chop Point

We have one point on either hand, on the outer edge opposite the thumb. We start by tapping on this point before moving on to the other meridians. It is the meridian associated with the small intestine, and an imbalance here can result in us feeling stuck and unable to move forward, which prevents us from being able to live in the moment and enjoy the here and now.

How to Perform an EFT Tapping Healing

The first step is to think about what it is you want to heal; it could be heartbreak, jealousy, shame, or anxiety. Remember, these negative feelings and emotions can all cause blockages in our spiritual selves.

Once you have identified the blockage, rate how it makes you feel on a scale of zero to ten, with zero being the lowest and ten being the extreme end of the scale. After you have finished your practice, you will rate it again, and this will help you gauge your process. The scale is unique to you, and no one can tell you how extreme an impact your emotions have, or where on a scale they should go. Generally, we are aiming to bring our emotions down to at least a three on the scale, preferably a zero.

Next, think of a statement or a mantra to repeat whilst you tap. It needs to be a statement that both acknowledges the issue and accepts it. Some examples include:

"I acknowledge my fear, and I accept it."
"I recognise my self-esteem issues and know that I am worthy of love."
"Even though I feel heartache, I give myself permission to feel and heal."

This statement is one of the most important elements of a successful EFT tapping session, so make sure that you take the time to create one that is perfectly aligned to your goal.

You will want to use four fingers when tapping. Start by tapping the karate chop point of the hand you aren't using. Repeat your statement out loud three times as you do so.

Once you have done this, take a deep breath. You will want to tap between five and seven times on the other points whilst focusing on your statement. Start with the eyebrow point, then the side of the eye points (using both hands, each point at the same time), then the under the eye points, then the under the nose point with one hand, followed by the chin point, the collarbone points with each hand simultaneously, then the underarm points, and finally one hand to tap the top of the head point.

Once you've finished, take another deep breath and think again on your issue. Do you feel any better? How would you rate it on your scale now, has there been any movement?

• • •

This is EFT tapping at its simplest. You will find that those more advanced in this healing method will use a different statement for each tapping point that corresponds with their overall goal, and there are entire scripts that can be found in books and online to help you perform a more in-depth session.

This method of healing requires some bravery, as it asks us to really delve into those emotions that are causing our blockages to allow us to heal from them. This can be painful, but there are several recommended approaches to doing so that can help.

My personal favourite is the storytelling technique, which is a common one in EFT tapping. Essentially, you recount the situation that you believe has led to this blockage to yourself as if you were telling the story to a third party. Let's say you had an argument with a partner, and they said some things that hurt. Imagine you are describing to a friend what happened; how the argument started, what they said, what you said. At any point during the story that you feel pain, anxiety, or discomfort, use that particular moment to create a statement and then begin tapping. Do not move on with the story until you rate this particular element of it as a two or three on the scale. You may not be able to finish the story in one sitting, and if you need to return to it then you can either start from the beginning or pick up from where you left off.

I will be honest; the EFT technique is not one that I tend to use that often, as I personally find I have better success with other methods. However, it is a popular method that many swear by, so give it a go and see how beneficial it is for you.

Chakras

There is a lot of information on chakras out there, with courses, books, and entire websites dedicated to the subject. As such, I'm going to be quite sparse with the details and won't be going into too much depth about the theory. Instead, I will be focusing on providing practical ways and exercises to help you work with your chakras. As I mentioned in the introduction, the chakras were my first taste of energy healing, and they have been a core part of my practice ever since.

The chakras have their origin in Sanskrit and are known as the energy centres of the body. There are seven main chakras that run from the base of the spine to the top of the head, and many other smaller chakras located within our bodies. You can find them in the hands, in the feet, and even outside of the body. However, for the purposes of this book, we will just be focusing on the seven main chakras.

These energy centres govern certain aspects of our physical, mental, emotional, and spiritual selves. They appear as spinning, coloured disks; the brighter and stronger they are, the healthier our energy is. When our chakras are blocked, we can experience a wealth of issues physically, mentally, emotionally, and spiritually. As such, it is important to keep your chakras healthy. You may think of chakras as "main" meridians, although remember that they are from different systems of belief, so this is more a comparison rather than a fact.

One element often overlooked in chakra work is that one blocked chakra can impact the other chakras. Chakras are often talked about in a singular way; for example, if you're feeling unmotivated to pursue your hobbies, then your sacral chakra must be blocked, as this governs our passions and interests. This is useful information when you are first starting out with chakra work as it helps you learn the main function of each chakra. However, as we all know, our problems are rarely that straightforward. In the example that I have given here, yes, the sacral chakra is the main chakra associated with our hobbies. But maybe you are feeling unmotivated to practice your hobbies because whilst you have an idea of what you want to create, you don't know how to put it into practice. In this case, you should focus on the throat chakra along with the sacral chakra, as the throat chakra is associated with creative expression.

To give another example, perhaps you are having money troubles and are worried about paying your rent. In this instance, the root chakra would be the most obvious chakra to work with, as it is associated with stability. However, it may be that you are struggling to make the calls you need to make or take the action you need to in order to manage your money issues. In this instance, it may be wise to work with the solar plexus chakra, which governs confidence, along with the root chakra.

Remember that these energy points are all connected to one another, and very rarely function independently. Once you are familiar with the basic functions of each chakra and delve deeper into working with each, you will begin to understand this connection on a more profound level. This will allow you to map the flow of energy through each chakra more clearly and recognise the combination of chakras you may need to work with to truly help you heal from those blockages.

For each chakra, I will give a bit of insight as to the associations of that chakra and touch on what you may experience if this chakra is blocked. I will then list crystals and scents that are associated with that chakra, and ways in which you can work with this chakra to open it, including the sound attributed to each chakra. I mirror this format for each of the chakras, so I do apologise if it feels a little repetitive, but it is all relevant information you can use to guide you if you choose to work with the chakras.

Advanced Chakra Work

Once you are familiar with the seven main chakras, can map the flow of energy through each, and have a working understanding as to how they are connected and impact one another, you may wish to advance your practice. As I mentioned, there are hundreds of chakras inside and outside of the body. In addition, different traditions will also work with different chakra systems; for example, in some branches of Buddhism they believe there are five chakras that connect three different channels in the body. If you are looking to expand beyond these seven, then I recommend researching the following:

The Earth Star Chakra—This chakra is said to link us to the earth's life force. It is located between our feet and the earth.

The Soul Star Chakra—Said to be the seat of the soul and where our life purpose resides. It is located about a foot above the head.

The Solar Star (or Spirit Star) Chakra—Opening this chakra will allow us to communicate with beings of higher power (such as angels and guides). It is located above the soul star chakra.

The Galactic Chakra—Opening this chakra allows us to travel to other dimensions and planes of existence. It is an energy field that is formed around us.

The Divine Gateway Chakra—Activating this chakra allows us to become one with the divine energy. This chakra is also considered to be an energy field around us.

Please note that these additional chakras are considered a Western addition to the chakra system and not the classic system from which the following seven chakras were adopted.

The Root Chakra

The root chakra is the first chakra we start with out of the seven main chakras. Its Sanskrit name is *Muladhara*, although it is also sometimes referred to as just *Adhara*. It is associated with the colour red, and it is located at the base of the spine.

The word *Muladhara* comes from *Mula* meaning "root" and *Adhara* meaning "support" or "base." It is the foundation of our being, which allows us to ground into ourselves and into the earth, providing us with stability and security. Our most basic needs, such as food, shelter, water, and the need for emotional fulfillment, all come from the root chakra. It governs our survival and our ability to adapt and survive. It is also said to be the seat of our ancestral memories, where the knowledge of our forebears and our past lives reside, which helps us connect with our roots.

The root chakra helps us find our independence, to be self-sufficient and rely on ourselves. Strengthening it can be useful for those who find they tend to rely on others to help them find direction, or who seem to go along with what everyone else says or does. It encourages us to think of ourselves, what is best for us, and to look after ourselves.

The root chakra is associated with the element of earth. Physically, it is associated with the skeletal structure, teeth, large intestine, kidneys, and blood. It is believed that strengthening the root chakra will also strengthen these physical aspects of ourselves.

When this chakra becomes blocked, we can experience anxiety and fear, feeling out of our depth like a little fish in the big sea. We can feel lost, overwhelmed, and anxious; merely surviving the day can feel like a massive undertaking. It can cause us to lose our connection with the earth and with others. Our relationships no longer feel like equal partnerships, but instead we begin to feel overly dependent on others. It can cause us to put the needs of others before ourselves, which in turn can lead to insecurity and self-doubt.

To stimulate and open the root chakra, you could try any red crystals and some darker coloured, such as brown or black, which are suitable for helping to cleanse and open this chakra. Good crystals to try include red carnelian, red jasper (my personal go-to for this chakra), black tourmaline, and obsidian. Try lying down, placing one of these over the root chakra, and visualising the energy of the crystal cleansing and strengthening your aura.

The sense of smell is strongly associated with the root chakra, so oils and other scents are great for stimulating the root chakra. Oils you could use include cedarwood, frankincense, patchouli, and sandalwood (remember; always dilute oils, never apply them neat).

As the root chakra is associated with our roots, you could also perform the roots meditation from the "grounding and centring" section in chapter 2, but instead visualise your roots coming out and down from your root chakra area. Then focus on pulling energy up through the earth and into your root chakra to help cleanse and empower it.

I always recommend using mantras to help with the chakras. Examples of those that you could use for your root chakra include:

> "I embrace my independence and have the strength to survive whatever I encounter along this path today."
>
> "I am strong and stable, safe and secure."
>
> "My roots are strong, my chakra balanced. I am immovable."

Each chakra also has a specific sound associated with it. You can help to open the chakras by chanting their sound out loud, focusing on the vibrations of the sound raising the chakra's energy levels. The sound for the root chakra is "LAM." You will notice as we go through the chakras that they all have very similar sounds "LAM," "VAM," YAM," so try to put some emphasis on the "L" as you sound it out.

The Sacral Chakra

The sacral chakra is the second chakra we focus on out of the seven main chakras. Its Sanskrit name is *Svadhisthana*. It is associated with the colour orange, and it is located above our root chakra and just below the belly button. It is the chakra of emotion, feeling in a physical sense (sensation), and expression of sexual desire.

The sacral chakra governs how we relate to others and to the world. It also governs where we fit in and encourages the expansion of self. It helps us to see "our place" in the world and feel comfortable in it. The word *Svadhisthana* means "your own place."

This chakra is sometimes called the foundation of our well-being. It encourages positive and harmonious interactions with those around us and allows us to manage the flow of our emotions in a healthy manner.

The sacral chakra is also associated with fantasy and creativity and governs our imagination and expression. The motivation to pursue our hobbies comes from the sacral chakra, whether those hobbies are physical, such as running or climbing, or more creative, such as scrapbooking or painting.

When this chakra becomes blocked, we can experience unhealthy codependency. Unlike the root chakra, where this codependency comes from feeling disconnected with ourselves, this blockage can make us feel disconnected with others. This can lead us to doing whatever we can to please others around us, as if that is the only way to establish a connection with others.

We may feel emotionally out of control and express those emotions to others in ways that are unhealthy. Or we could experience the other end of the scale and find ourselves completely uninterested and numb to the world, and the people, around us.

Another sign that this chakra is blocked is overindulging in fantasies or obsessions and looking for ways to "escape" the world around us (this includes addiction to substances that give us that temporary release). Again, however, we may find the opposite: an absolute lack of creativity and imagination.

To stimulate and open the sacral chakra, you could try any orange crystals, which are suitable for helping to cleanse and open this chakra. Good crystals to place upon this point and visualise their energy healing your chakra include sunstone, goldstone, amber (which I recommend using if you wish to focus on creativity), and orange carnelian (an especially good crystal if you wish to focus on building positive relationships with others).

There are several oils and scents associated with the sacral chakra, including sweet orange, cinnamon, cardamom, and ylang-ylang.

As the sacral chakra is associated with movement, physical exercise can also help. Yoga, pilates, or any other practice that really focuses on "being in" your body can have a benefit if you focus on opening this chakra whilst you are performing these exercises.

If, like me, you are a fan of mantras, here are some you may wish to try to help stimulate the sacral chakra:

"I love all aspects of myself and celebrate the best of me."

"I am the creator of my own reality and control my own destiny."

"I am connected to the ebb and flow of all life and find joy as it flows through me."

Help open the sacral chakra by chanting its sound out loud, focusing on the vibrations of the sound raising the chakra's energy levels. The sound for the sacral chakra is "VAM."

Solar Plexus Chakra

The solar plexus chakra is the third chakra out of the seven main chakras. Its Sanskrit name is *Manipura*. It is associated with the colour yellow, and it is located above the belly button and below the rib cage.

Whereas the sacral chakra helps us focus on our place in the world and our relationship with it, the solar plexus focuses on our will and our personal power. It helps us take control of our lives and take responsibility for our actions and decisions. It helps us in making those decisions and can bring clarity to our lives, helping us form and feel comfortable in our thoughts and opinions.

Self-assurance, confidence, and independence are associated with this chakra. It can help us determine our personal identity. It can also help us to practise self-discipline where it is needed.

The solar plexus chakra also governs our mental abilities. It can help us be more organised, assessing the positives and negatives in life, and generally help us feel more on top of things.

Drawing on all of these attributes, this chakra can help us to establish our plans and ideas into reality, and at a high level, can even convey wisdom.

When this chakra becomes blocked, we can experience an unhealthy attitude toward authority and control; either wanting too much of it or relinquishing all responsibility and being unable to accept the consequences of our actions. You may even find yourself manipulating those around you or misusing any power you have.

Becoming obsessed with minor details, lacking clear direction (especially in regard to the bigger picture), or making plans but then never knowing how to follow through with them, are also signs that this chakra is blocked.

To stimulate and open the solar plexus chakra, you could try any the colour yellow. Yellow crystals are suitable for helping to cleanse and open this chakra. Good crystals to try include citrine (which is especially good for increasing joy), tiger's eye (a great one to use if you wish to focus on building your confidence), and yellow tourmaline.

If you wish to incorporate oils and scents into your practice to help strengthen this chakra, then good ones to try include lemon balm, fennel, and black pepper.

As the solar plexus is considered the seat of our personal power, taking the time to reflect on your achievements can also help to strengthen this chakra. Take a moment at the end of the day to think upon and celebrate your successes. They may be small, such as "I finally did the washing up today." Recognizing your achievements helps build confidence, which can improve our sense of self and help us connect to our personal power, thus empowering our solar plexus chakra.

If you wish to try mantras, here are some examples of those appropriate for the solar plexus chakra:

"I am a confident individual. I take control of my life and the path that I walk."

"My mind is sharp, and I approach the world with the intelligence to learn and grow."

"I am decisive and take responsibility for the outcomes of my actions with strength and confidence."

Help open the solar plexus chakra by chanting its sound out loud, focusing on the vibrations of the sound raising the chakra's energy levels. The sound for the solar plexus chakra is "RAM."

Heart Chakra

The heart chakra is considered the fourth of the main chakras. Its Sanskrit name is *Anahata*. It is associated with the colour green, and it is located in the centre of the chest.

Unsurprisingly, the heart chakra focuses on emotions such as compassion, forgiveness, and overcoming grief. It can help us feel love for ourselves, feel love for others, and develop deeper and more meaningful relationships. It can teach us compassion and empathy for others and the world around us. It can help us to forgive, to accept, and to move on as we heal. However, balancing this chakra can also help us to still view situations and people objectively and with clarity, just with more compassion in general.

The heart chakra also governs transformation and change. Often change can be unwelcome and unwanted. This chakra will help you come to terms with, and deal with, significant change, whether that change comes externally or from within. It is an especially good chakra to focus on for those who are grieving. It can help us accept what has been lost and find peace within ourselves.

When this chakra becomes blocked, we can experience a range of negative emotions, such as defensiveness and anger. We can start to develop a "victim complex," or at the opposite end of the scale, a "saviour complex."

We could also experience the need for codependency, but on the opposite end of the scale. It could force us to become too isolated and unwilling or not wanting to socialise or get close to others.

Finally, a blockage in this chakra can manifest in holding on to grudges or feelings of jealousy and envy, and can prevent you from letting go or moving on from negative moments in your life.

To stimulate and open the heart chakra, you could try any green or pink crystals, which are suitable for helping to cleanse and open this chakra.

Rose quartz is my go-to crystal for the heart chakra, but other crystals you could use include bloodstone (especially good for drawing out negativity caused by jealousy and similar emotions), malachite, and green aventurine (a great all-rounder).

Oils and scents you could use to stimulate the heart chakra include rose, lavender, and jasmine.

With the heart chakra being the seat of love and compassion, you can use affirmative actions to help open this chakra. Set the intention to perform one small, random act of kindness today, and dedicate it to your heart chakra to help raise its vibration.

You can chant mantras designed to help stimulate and strengthen your heart chakra. Examples of these are:

"I accept love into my heart, and I give love freely."

"May my eyes see the beauty of the world around me, and my heart be open to the love in this world around me."

"I acknowledge my [insert specific feeling here, such as anger, jealousy, grief, etc.]. I accept it and move on from it. It leaves me now."

Help open the heart chakra by chanting its sound out loud, focusing on the vibrations of the sound raising the chakra's energy levels. The sound for the heart chakra is "YAM."

Throat Chakra

The throat chakra is the fifth chakra in the main chakra system. Its Sanskrit name is *Vishuddha*. It is associated with the colour blue, and it is located at the centre of the neck.

As you may expect, the throat chakra focuses on communication and expression. This communication can be verbal or non-verbal, externally to other people, or even internally to yourself.

With communication comes self-expression. As well as helping you actually communicate with others and with yourself, this chakra can help you improve the way you express yourself via that communication. It can assist if you often find yourself in situations where you find it difficult to be truthful for whatever reason, or to speak up for yourself. It can also help you find the words and expressions you need to accurately get your point across.

The throat chakra isn't just about communication here in the physical realm but can also assist us in communicating with the spirit world and "other" worlds.

The throat chakra can also help us express our creativity. It focuses on helping us to project those ideas we've had into reality, so we can start realising them.

I have found that, because of its location, blockages here can result in bottlenecks, which can then affect the flow of energy to your other chakras. Opening this chakra can therefore help you to open and balance your other chakras by allowing this energy to flow more freely.

It is often an underappreciated chakra, especially in terms of its influence on other chakras. For example, you may work with your heart chakra to help you feel more compassionate and in touch with your emotions, but how helpful is that if you can't communicate your emotions effectively? We may work with our solar plexus chakra to increase our confidence and independence, but we also need to be able to communicate this confidence to really benefit from it. As such, working with the throat chakra can have a positive impact on your other chakras too.

When this chakra becomes blocked, it is our communication that can suffer the most. You may find yourself too afraid to speak up or unable to find the words you need. On the opposite end of the scale, you may find that you talk too much, and your words are jumbled or nonsensical, or that you have difficulties listening to others because you're just focused on getting your "say" in.

You may also find yourself susceptible to lying or find that you are unable to keep secrets and find pleasure in gossiping about others.

To stimulate and open the throat chakra, you could try any blue crystals, which are suitable for helping to cleanse and open this chakra. Good crystals to try include blue lace agate (often associated with creativity), aquamarine, sodalite (great for communication in general), and turquoise (which I recommend for improving your confidence in your communication skills).

Oils and scents associated with the throat chakra include peppermint, vanilla, eucalyptus, and chamomile.

With the throat chakra being focused on communication, writing a poem or a song and reciting it/singing it can help open this chakra. If you don't feel like creating your own, then feel free to use something someone else has written, but it will be stronger if you use your own creative expression.

As with all chakras, you can try mantras designed to help stimulate and strengthen your throat chakra. Examples of these include:

> "My words are strong and true, and spoken with love."
>
> "I speak with truth and listen with openness."
>
> "I will speak when I have something worth saying, and all will listen."

Help open the throat chakra by chanting its sound out loud, focusing on the vibrations of the sound raising the chakra's energy levels. The sound for the throat chakra is "HAM."

Third Eye Chakra

The third eye chakra is considered the sixth chakra. Its Sanskrit name is *Ajna*. It is associated with the colour purple, and it is located between the eyebrows.

The third eye chakra is the seat of our intuition and foresight. It is associated with all things psychic and can help improve our abilities in all psychic practices. When we practise scrying or divination techniques (in order to help us understand our inner selves and/or the future), it is often through the third eye chakra that we receive our visions.

The third eye chakra helps us see the unseen including different planes of existence, spirits, and so forth. It can help us move beyond the bounds of the physical realm and communicate with guides, spirits, and such. Opening this chakra can help us recognise the subtle shifts in energy all around us, and so it is a good chakra for those who practise energy work or healing especially.

The third eye chakra is also the chakra of wisdom and intellect, helping us to learn and grow from these spiritual experiences. This focus on spirituality can also help inspire profound creative ideas and works on a higher level.

Whilst there isn't too much to say on the third eye chakra that can't be covered in just a few paragraphs, the stretch to which its influence reaches should not be underestimated. Our day-to-day intuition and gut instinct are associated with this chakra. That sense of foreboding you receive just before something goes wrong… that voice in your head that tells you to take a different route home than the one you were planning… or the instinct not to trust a certain person? All ruled by this chakra. As well as affecting our higher, spiritual selves, working on this chakra can have deep, "every day" significance too.

When this chakra becomes blocked, you may find that you just lose touch with your spirituality completely. You get "stuck" in the daily grind, with no thought for the spiritual self. Or you may find that you become overly dependent on material possessions, relying on those for your happiness.

Lack of "vision," the inability to set long-term goals, and only being able to consider what feels best for you at that very moment are also signs that your third eye chakra is blocked.

To stimulate and open the third eye chakra, use any purple crystals, which are suitable for helping to cleanse and open this chakra. Good crystals to try include amethyst (generally associated with intuition), fluorite (especially purple fluorite), lapis lazuli, and labradorite.

If you wish to try different oils and scents to stimulate this chakra, then bay laurel, juniper, and frankincense are all great ones to try.

Yoga, Qi Gong, or any form of "moving meditation" (and just regular meditation) can help strengthen the third eye chakra; even just a short, ten-minute routine can help.

If you wish to incorporate mantras into your work with the third eye chakra, then you could try these:

"I am in tune with my higher self; I am guided by my intuition."

"My sight sees beyond this world, and I walk with the seen and the unseen."

"I listen to my inner voice, and let my higher self guide me."

Help open the third eye chakra by chanting its sound out loud, focusing on the vibrations of the sound raising the chakra's energy levels. The sound for the third eye chakra is "OHM."

The Crown Chakra

The crown chakra is the seventh, and final, chakra in the main chakra system. Its Sanskrit name is *Sahasrara*. Its colour is white, (although it is sometimes depicted as violet; I personally feel better able to connect with it when using white). The crown chakra is located at the top of the head.

This chakra is the seat of our spiritual power, or our divine journey. Working with this chakra allows us to connect with a higher consciousness and recognise and feel a part of all that is sacred.

It helps us release limiting patterns and is often used in energy healing. In my reiki training, I was taught that this is the first chakra we focus on opening. Often when we are calling upon healing energy, we visualise it entering our body through the crown chakra. In a way, you transcend the "every day" and see past the mundane, recognising the spiritual essence in all things. We feel at one with everything in the universe, truly connected to this universal energy, and find peace within this existence.

There isn't too much else to say on the crown chakra; so few sentences sum up what truly is a life-changing chakra!

When this chakra becomes blocked, you may find that you feel disconnected to the universe and universal energy, the Divine, Source, and develop a cynicism for the sacred. Closed-mindedness and an attachment to the material world or the need to fill your life with material possessions may also manifest if there are issues with the crown chakra.

On the opposite end of the scale, if this chakra is too open, then you may experience a sense of being disconnected to your body and the physical world around you.

To stimulate and open the crown chakra, you could try any white crystals. Good crystals to try include clear quartz (a great amplifier of energy), selenite, opal, and Botswana agate (recommended to me by a fellow reiki practitioner, and one which I can't get enough of).

Oils and scents you could use to stimulate the crown chakra include rose, lotus, jasmine, and frankincense.

Spiritual practices such as meditation are a great way of connecting with your higher self and empowering this chakra further, especially if you focus specifically on this chakra during those meditations.

If you wish to use mantras to help open this chakra, then examples of ones you could use include:

"I am connected to the universe and to the Divine."

"I walk in the sacred light of the Spirit, and work for the highest good."

"I am at one with the universal energy; it flows through me and connects me to the all."

Help open the crown chakra by chanting its sound out loud, focusing on the vibrations of the sound raising the chakra's energy levels. The sound for the crown chakra is "ANG."

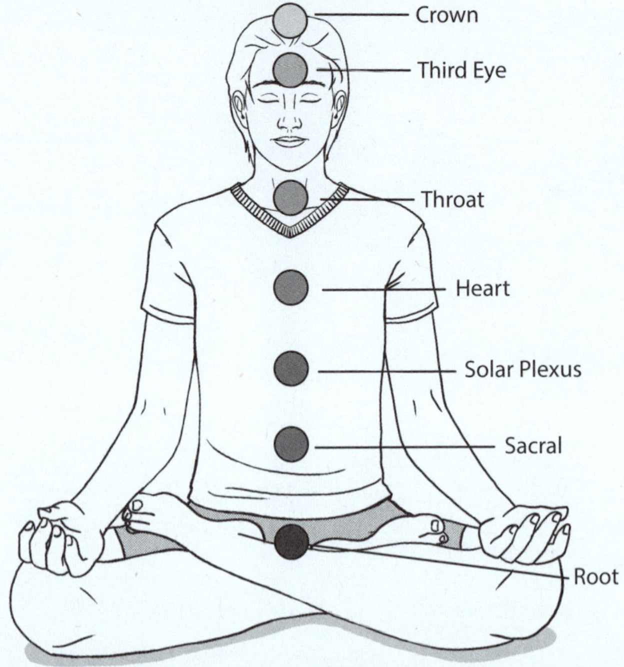

Figure 14: The 7 Main Chakra Points

Performing a Chakra Energy Scan

One of the best ways to "check in" with your chakras is to perform the energy scanning technique we discussed in the "preparing for energy healing" section at the beginning of this chapter.

Perform the scan and, as you bring your hands down your body, pause at each chakra point. What do you feel, see, or sense? Can you sense the colour of each chakra, and if so, what shade is it (the lighter and brighter, the healthier the chakra)? Can you sense it spinning, and if so, is it moving fast, slow, or at a steady pace (fast indicates energy overload, whilst slowly can indicate a lack of energy)? Do any words or feelings pop into your head? Remember, everyone senses energy in their own way, and the idea is to figure out how you sense it and how you read it.

• • •

Below are two meditations you can use to help strengthen and empower your chakras. The first meditation is very much a "light touch" version—very quick and simple; I have found that even just five or ten minutes a day with this one can make a difference. The second is a bit more in-depth and intense, and it is a good one to perform once a month.

Meditation One: Quick Chakra Empowerment

This is a very simple meditation that relies on visualisation and can be used when you want to give your chakras a quick boost. Simply sit somewhere comfortably and enter meditation in whatever way suits you best.

Focus on connecting with your energy. You may wish to perform the energy orb exercise, the roots meditation, breathing exercises, or the centring exercise earlier on in this book.

Now, inhale. As you do, imagine the breath entering your body as golden energy. Follow this breath as it travels down your body, collecting in your power centre.

When you exhale, see this golden light expanding through your body, through each of your chakras. This light pulsates with a strong, healing energy that fills each chakra. From your crown to your root, each one glows brighter and brighter. Eventually, see this light expanding out past your body, forming a shimmering, golden bubble around you, similar to the energy shield. This pure, golden light is divine healing of the highest power, cleansing your chakras of all negativity, strengthening them with its essence.

See this bubble wrapping around you, feeding your chakras with every exhale. Know that this shield will continue to protect and strengthen your chakras as you go about your day-to-day business. Then, finish the meditation when you feel ready to.

Meditation Two: Chakra Cleanse Meditation

This meditation requires chanting out loud; as we are relying on the vibrations of the sounds we will be making. It will not be as effective if performed in silence.

Step One: Opening Your Chakras

Prepare for meditation in whatever way suits you best.

Start with the root chakra and imagine it slowly opening up like an eye. See it glowing with a bright red light as it opens.

Do this with the remaining chakras, working your way up; an orange light for your sacral, yellow for your solar plexus, green for your heart, blue for your throat, purple for your third eye, and white for your crown.

Step 2: Cleansing Your Chakras

Now, above your head see a ball of bright white light. This is the light of the universal energy, pure and working for the highest good. Its supply is limitless, so you can take as much as you want, and it will never run out.

See this light pouring down from the ball, and starting with your crown chakra, see it filling that chakra. Visualise it consuming any negative energy you may be holding in that chakra (I usually see this negative energy as black flecks or spots), growing brighter and stronger until all that negativity is gone. See this light then overflowing from your crown chakra, cascading down to your third eye chakra, and then repeat the process with that chakra.

Do this for each of your chakras, working your way down to the root chakra.

Step 3: Strengthening Your Chakras

For this we are going to be using the specific sounds for each chakra; make sure you have these in front of you. It can be difficult to remember, so if you need to open your eyes to remind yourself of them throughout the meditation, then feel free to do so. As you chant the sounds, see or feel the vibration of the sound permeating your chakra, making the light shine brighter and stronger.

Start with the root chakra, and chant "LLLAAAAAMM" three times.

Move to the sacral chakra, and chant "VVVAAAAAMM" three times.

Move to the solar plexus, and chant "RRRAAAAAMM" three times.

Move to the heart chakra, and chant "YYYAAAAAMM" three times.

Move to the throat chakra, and chant "HHHAAAAAMM" three times.

Move to the third eye chakra, and chant "OOOHHHHHMM" three times.

Move to the crown chakra, and chant "AAANNNNNGG" three times.

Finally, go back down to the root chakra and chant the corresponding sound just once. Repeat this with the sacral once, the solar plexus, the heart, the throat, the third eye and the crown.

Step 4: Closing the Chakras

Visualise a giant zip, starting at your groin area and running up your body. It is currently open, the teeth of the zipper running up either side of your chakras.

Now, mentally pull this zip up past your root chakra. See your root chakra zipping up, closing completely, your chakra energy now being stored within your body.

Keep pulling the zip up and see this closing each chakra in turn in the same way, right up past your crown chakra, to the top of your head. It is important to make sure that we close our chakras; this can help prevent negative energy from seeping in but also stop our energy from "leaking" out. Trust that they will still be working beneath your skin, keeping you energised and empowered.

Auras

The aura is an etheric energy field that surrounds each person. It is made of energy and is connected with our own energy. As such, the aura reflects our thoughts, feelings, and emotions.

The energy of our aura reaches out between 2 and 3 feet from our bodies, and so we interact with others' auras on a daily basis. Have you ever come into contact with someone and just got a "bad feeling," or met a stranger and had that instant connection? This is due to that energetic signature they are giving off (their aura). For those who are sensitive to energy, you will probably find you pick up the "first impressions" of a person before they have even opened their mouth, more so than those who aren't attuned to this energy.

By understanding auras, how they work, and how to work with them, you can learn to recognise where energy blockages may be lurking in yourself and others, so you can then work toward healing them. There are two main "schools of thought" when it comes to auras. Some believe that the aura is just an overall energy field that contains many different colours all intermingled with one another in a kaleidoscope of different shades and patterns. These colours indicate the general well-being of a person.

Some believe that the aura is a bit more structured. In this instance, the aura contains seven layers and each of these is connected with one of the seven chakras. The "state" of a person will determine which layer shines through the brightest. As I briefly mentioned at the beginning of the book, I have met several people who believe in auras but not the chakra system. The information I'm laying out here is not what I believe to be "the one right way," and I won't tell you it's my way or the highway, as that would very much go against the ethos of this book. However, as I work closely with the chakras, I do personally see the aura as connected to them. So, take this information and use it so you can be well informed and develop a practice that fits your personal experience and beliefs.

Let's take a look at the seven layers of the aura and how they are connected to the chakras.

The Seven Auric Layers

Layer 1: The Etheric Layer—This layer is closest to the body and is connected to the root chakra. It is generally said to be a blue-grey colour, and the more physically active a person is, the stronger this layer will appear.

Layer 2: The Emotional Layer—This layer is second from the body. It is connected with the sacral chakra and is associated with emotions and feelings. It is said to be pretty much any colour. The more stressed a person is feeling, the weaker this layer will appear.

Layer 3: The Mental Layer—This layer is third from the body and is connected with the solar plexus chakra. It is associated with our thoughts, our intellect, and cognitive processes. It is said that it is bright yellow in colour. This layer appears strongest when the person is engaging in mental or creative activities.

Layer 4: The Astral Layer—This layer is fourth from the body. It is connected with the heart chakra and is associated with our relationships with others and acts as a bridge between the physical and spiritual. It is said to be pink in colour, and it becomes stronger through intimate and loving relationships.

Layer 5: The Etheric Template—This layer is fifth from the body. It is connected with the throat chakra and is associated with our physical selves; our identity, personality, and general energy and can be pretty much any colour. This layer appears at its strongest in those who are truthful and comfortable enough to express themselves.

Layer 6: The Celestial Layer—This layer is sixth from the body. It is connected with the third eye chakra and is associated with our connection to the Divine, our connection to our spiritual selves, and unconditional love. It is white in colour, and this layer appears at its strongest in those connected with the spirit world.

Layer 7: The Keteric Layer—This layer is the farthest away from the body and is connected with the crown chakra. It represents our highest selves and connection with the universe. It is gold in colour and appears at its strongest in those who have that strong connection with the universe.

The Colours of the Aura

It can be difficult to see the individual layers of a person's aura, especially the outer layers. When you view someone's aura, you may "see" one colour more strongly than the others, or you may see a combination of colours that can help in "reading" a person. The specific shade of the colour is also an important indicator as to the state of a person's well-being.

As the aura is an energetic representation of us, and we are constantly in flux, so too is our aura. Whilst the colours representing the layers do not change, they can change in the shade of that colour or they can be weaker or stronger. As our energy changes, so does our aura. What you are looking for is the most prominent colours and their specific shade. The following is just a brief overview of some of the colours that can be found in the auric field and what each of the colours symbolise.

Red—This colour has the lowest vibrational frequency of any of the other colours and so is closely associated with the physical. People whose aura shows red as the most dominant colour tend to be those who are physically very fit and active and take care of their physical selves. They are passionate, motivated, and adventurous. A murkier red can indicate that the person is feeling low on physical energy or feeling physically overwhelmed, or that they are holding on to anger.

Orange—This colour indicates a childlike attitude. These people are sociable, outgoing, and love the company of others. People whose aura shows a strong orange colour as the most dominant colour are energetic and have a "zest for life." A murkier orange can indicate that someone has trouble committing in their relationships.

Yellow—This colour symbolises the intellect as well as our personal power. Those whose aura is a strong yellow colour are great leaders who naturally inspire others with their confidence and their optimism. They are also very intelligent and enjoy any activity that engages the brain. A murkier yellow can indicate that someone is lacking in confidence or engaging in negative self-talk, or perhaps overconfident in their abilities and too focused on perfection.

Green—Green is associated with healing, personal growth, and nature. Those whose aura is primarily a strong green colour tend to be quite nurturing, feeling a need to support those around them. They have a strong connection to nature and are generally quite calm and relaxed people. A murkier green can indicate someone who is maybe selfish, experiencing feelings of jealousy or envy, or is taking criticism too harshly and seeing themselves as a victim.

Blue—This colour is associated with intuition, spirituality, communication, and creativity. Those whose aura is primarily a strong blue colour are very spiritually in tune with themselves and the world around them, or they are quite creative individuals and are generally strong communicators. A murkier blue can indicate that someone is out of touch with the spiritual self, or that they are someone who struggles to communicate and feels like they can't express their true thoughts or selves.

Violet—This colour is associated with the Divine, open-mindedness, and progression. Those whose aura is primarily a strong violet colour tend to be very forward thinking and socially progressive. They strongly believe that there is more to life than the material and tend to shun what they see as shallow or materialistic pursuits.

They are empaths and sensitive to the energy around them, using their intuition to help see the truth in all situations. Often there is a sense that they are a part of "something bigger." A murkier violet colour can indicate that someone is disillusioned with the world around them, or that they are struggling to keep up with a changing world around them and feeling a lot of self-doubt.

Pink—Pink is said to be quite a rare colour to see in an aura. Where it does appear, it can indicate that the person in question has a great balance between the material and the spiritual. They are romantic and gentle, comforting, and uplifting.

White—With white being associated with the crown chakra, it is the one farthest away from the body and so can also be quite rare to see in someone. You may see flecks of white in someone's aura, but it is very unlikely that white will be the most dominant colour. If it is the most dominant colour, it denotes a person of great spiritual connection.

Gold—Gold is associated with divine energy, and those who have a primarily strong golden aura are usually very connected to the divine energies and universe around them.

How to See Auras

There are some people who can physically see auras, as well as sense them energetically. The best way is to start by trying to see your own aura. If you are successful in this, you can move on to viewing the auras of other people.

One of the most effective ways of viewing your own aura is to grab a large-ish mirror—one you can easily see yourself from the chest up in—and sit in front of a white wall with the mirror in front of you. A white wall provides a neutral background.

Focus on your shoulders and head and soften your vision, effectively "zoning out." Your vision should become blurry as you stop focusing on anything physical or tangible. Before long, you should start to see colours encircling you—I personally view them more strongly around the top of the head. If you do start to see colours, don't focus too hard on them; make a mental note of the colours, and let them flow. What colours can you see? Are they light, dark, do they change quickly?

Also make a note as to whether the aura is a complete field, or whether there are any gaps or "breaks" in it. I have heard of some people who read auras reporting that they occasionally see breaks in the aura, and this is often representative of a physical injury in that particular part of the body. The more you practise this exercise, the more adept you will become. You may find yourself seeing these breaks or patterns, which can tell you more about a person's state.

When you are done, record your findings, as well as your interpretation of them, in a journal. This is a great exercise to practise at least once a week to give you an idea as to how the aura can change and how the colours can be influenced by our physical, mental, and emotional states.

The more you practise, the easier it will become, and once you feel comfortable with this you can start trying to see another's aura. Use the same technique but just focus on someone else. It can be a little trickier to practice—unless you have some very good friends. They may be a bit weirded out if you ask them to just stand in front of a white wall! But with enough practice, your surroundings will matter less and less when it comes to viewing auras.

You may not "see" auras at all but instead experience them in a different way. Remember, not everyone experiences energy in the same way and what comes easy for one person might not be easy for the next person. In fact, most people tend to find it easier to "sense" auras rather than physically see them (and I am one of those people). You may instead get a feeling, such as one of optimism that could indicate a yellow aura. Or the word "yellow" may pop into your head. Maybe you hear sounds instead; a certain sound could indicate yellow, a different sound could indicate blue, and so on. So, pay attention to other sensations whilst you are performing this exercise and make a note of them in your journal to see if there are any patterns or themes, to help you better understand how you personally experience auras.

How to Heal, Strengthen, and Protect Your Aura

Once you have an understanding as to what auras are and how to sense them, you can work on healing and strengthening yours and others, and also making sure you are keeping yours well protected against everyday negativity. There are several benefits to healing and strengthening your aura: you can ensure you are protected against negative energies and overcome trauma and negative thought patterns that create energetic blockages. One of the main benefits, in my opinion, is being able to use your aura to draw specific energies toward you by raising and strengthening your own vibrational frequency.

One of the most influential names in the field of aura work is Edgar Cayce (1877–1945), and his work is still in use today. He would often read people's auras and then give them suggestions, often linked with colours, to aid them. For example, in one reading with a young woman who was often temperamental and judgmental, he recommended that she avoid wearing red, as this would accentuate these negative qualities. In another reading, he recommended a client wear more red to help her be more vibrant.[10] He recognised that different colours have different vibrational levels that could influence the energy of our aura, and so working with colour is an ideal way to help heal and strengthen your aura.

The primary way to do this is to "program" your energy, essentially feeding your aura with what it is you want to attain, very much in the spirit of "like attracts like." This is a surprisingly simple exercise, but it may take a bit of practice before you feel the results. Often healing is not a "one and

10. Mikao Usui and Frank Arjava Petter, *The Original Reiki Handbook of Dr. Mikao Usui: The Traditional Usui Reiki Ryoho Treatment Positions and Numerous Reiki Techniques for Health and Well-Being* (Lotus Press, 1999), Kindle.

done" activity (especially if your energy blockages are deeply rooted), even if the actual healing exercise is fairly straightforward. For example, do you feel you need to be more open and communicative? Do you want to feel more confident to express your true thoughts or feelings? Or do you need help healing from an argument you had with your partner?

Aura Programming Exercise

Find the colour that best suits your purpose. In the previous examples, you could choose blue for communication and self-expression or yellow for leadership. If you just wish to send general healing energy to the aura, then you may want to stick with white or even gold. Find somewhere you won't be disturbed and enter meditation in whatever way suits you best.

You will need to connect with your own energy. You should have a grasp as to how to do so by this point if you have read from the beginning (if not, then I recommend heading back to chapter 2).

When you have that connection, focus on flooding your aura with the light of your chosen colour. It can be useful to use your breath here. Visualise yourself inhaling energy of that colour, and then exhaling it out through your body. See it expanding out from within you, strong and radiant, filling your aura. Tell yourself that this is the colour your aura will glow most strongly, and you embody those qualities you are seeking. Do this for as long as you feel comfortable doing it for, and as often as you feel you need to, before you notice a difference.

• • •

You can always perform this for others if you wish to aid them in healing their own aura. If you do so, first determine what it is they need. You may do this by viewing their aura to understand where they may need assistance, or you can just ask them outright where they feel the focus should be. You can then use this information to understand the colour you should use.

If you do believe that auras are connected to the chakras, you could perform the body scanning exercise to understand which chakra has a blockage and use the colour that corresponds with that particular chakra in your healing. Focus on connecting with the aura of the person you are healing; I personally like to hold my hands out toward them and breathe the energy of the colour into myself, and then see this energy travelling out through my hands and into their aura. Focus again on flooding their aura with this particular colour, as you did for your own aura.

In terms of protecting your aura, any of the methods mentioned in chapter 1 will work. Personally, I recommend the shielding exercise, but make sure you visualise the shield encompassing your whole aura and not just your physical body.

Reiki

Reiki is a Japanese word that is formed of two parts. The first, *Rei*, means "universal." The second part, *Ki*, means "energy" or "life force energy." So, the word *reiki* itself means "universal energy" or "universal life force energy." According to the tale, Dr. Mikao Usui was the first to discover and document reiki. He went on a twenty-one-day retreat of meditation and fasting on Mount Kurama. On the twenty-first day, he felt this universal life force energy and the reiki symbols were revealed to him. By tapping into this energy and using these symbols, we can learn to energetically heal ourselves and others.

Reiki has five principles associated with it that those who practise try to live by. I often use the below version to help set me up for the day:

"Just for today, I will not worry.
Just for today, I will not anger.
Just for today, I will be humble.
Just for today, I will be honest.
Just for today, I shall show compassion to myself and others."

Usui Reiki

There are many different types of reiki. The form I personally work with, and am attuned to at "master" level, is Usui Reiki. There are three levels—levels 1, 2, and 3, with level 3 being "master"—that usually involve an attunement. An attunement is almost like an initiation ceremony that a reiki master performs on you. They will attune you to this universal life force energy and allow you to become a conduit of that energy so you can heal yourself and others. However, I personally see no reason why you can't use the principles of reiki healing on yourself without an attunement.

The important thing to remember with reiki is that it emphasises connecting with this universal life energy to perform it; you aren't using your own energy to heal but acting as that conduit. We have already encountered this technique during the exercises in chapter 2, so do please familiarise yourself with them if you wish to try reiki.

Usui Reiki often works with the chakras, which you should have a grasp of from the previous chakra section. It is interesting to note that incorporating the chakras is more of a Western addition to the reiki that Dr. Usui originally taught. Dr. Usui believed that energy should be channelled into the body through specific hand shapes, movements, tapping, and that energy would flow to where it needed to go. I personally find that the chakras provide a good focus point, especially when you are starting out. However, listening to your intuition and letting that guide you as to where to direct the energy is more closely aligned with Usui Reiki as it was originally taught. There are also the five reiki symbols that were revealed to Dr. Mikao Usui and are incorporated into the healing.[11] These symbols are:

Cho Ku Rei (The Power Symbol)—Often the first symbol taught, it increases the universal energy coming to you and is a good all-rounder in healing. Think of it as being a symbol that says "direct the energy here."

11. "Usui Reiki Symbols and Their Meanings," Centre of Excellence, accessed December 8, 2025, https://www.centreofexcellence.com/reiki-symbols-meanings/.

Sei Hei Ki (Emotional Symbol)—Focuses on emotional healing and clearing emotional blockages.

Hon Sha Ze Sho Nen (The Distance Symbol)—Strengthens your ability to heal from a distance and allows reiki to travel across space and time. As someone who mostly does distance healing, it is one I personally use a lot.

Dai Ko Myo (The Usui Master Symbol)—Helps call on the universal energy in your healing and can also help with spiritual growth. It is a great symbol to use to help cleanse and empower. As noted, it is considered the master symbol, and the most powerful. This symbol should only be used by reiki masters.

Raku (Grounding Symbol)—Used in the final stages of healing to help "seal" the energy in.

To use these, you need to draw the symbol associated with each with your dominant hand over the person you are healing, and visualise the symbol being drawn in the light of the universal energy. Then see this energy seeping into the recipient, fusing with their own energy, and working its power on their own energy field. I also personally like to trace the Cho Ku Rei symbol on my palms before a session, to help me better attune to healing energy.

Hands On Versus Hands Off

There are two ways I have been taught to perform a reiki session. The first is by using specific hand placements over the body where they correspond with the chakras. This is generally a "hands on" method, where you are actively touching the client. These hand shapes align more with Dr. Usui's original teachings.

I personally prefer to perform "hands off" reiki sessions, where I place my hands just above the body. I find that this is generally more comfortable for myself and the client, and so I do not use the traditional hand placements and won't be including them here.

Performing a Reiki Healing Session

To perform a reiki healing, perform the following steps—these are relevant whether you are healing yourself or someone else and whether you are doing an in-person or distance healing. I am using the chakras in this example because, as I stated previously, I do think that they provide more of a structured focus for beginners to reiki. I also deliberately don't include the use of the reiki symbols, as I believe that it is best to have formal training and have been attuned before you use these.

Step 1: Plan out what you want to achieve with your healing. Is this a general healing to cleanse and empower your chakras, or is there anything specifically that needs working on? If there is something specific, which symbols do you think are best to use and which chakras do you think you should focus on? If there is something specific, which chakras do you think you should focus on?

Step 2: Make sure the person you are healing (or yourself) is comfortable. I tend to perform self-healings whilst sitting down with my back against a wall, but when I am performing reiki on other people or receiving it from someone myself, I prefer to have them lie down/lie down myself. Maybe you could burn some incense or put on some calming music.

Step 3: Perform the energy orb exercise from chapter 2 to help you feel the energy.

Step 4: Clear your mind and attune to the universal energy by visualising a bright white light above you. This is the universal energy that shines down through you; tap into this, know it is pure and healing and will aid you in your highest workings. Take this energy into your body using any of the methods we have previously discussed. I like to use my breath and focus on taking this energy into my body as I inhale, before seeing it as a waterfall of light that constantly flows into my body through my crown chakra.

Step 5: Perform the scanning exercise from the "preparing for healing" section on the person you are healing to help you further identify where you may need to put extra energy in.

Step 6: Starting at the crown chakra, visualise it opening—or you may even wish to use your hands to mimic opening the chakra, as you would a book.

Step 7: Move your hands down the body, hovering slightly above it, and repeat this for each of the chakras. As always, listen to your intuition and let the energy guide you. Maybe you feel drawn to a particular area and want to spend a bit of time sending healing energy there? Focus on seeing that healing reiki energy flowing into your body, through you, and out into the chakras of your recipient as you move your hands down their body.

Step 8: When you are done, stand back and visualise the recipient glowing with this pure, healing energy as they radiate this light.

Step 9: Return to the crown chakra and now close it—again, through visualisation or even using your hands as if you were now closing a book—and see this energy now encapsulated in their body.

Step 10: State your thanks to the universe for allowing you to use this healing energy in your session.

If you are performing a long-distance healing on someone, I recommend at least having a conversation with them beforehand, to help you attune to their energy. I've performed distance healing for people that I have only spoken to through messages online that have been successful—it is entirely possible to perform a healing on someone without ever meeting them. When it comes to doing the healing, you can connect with their energy and visualise them lying in front of you, performing the steps above at the appropriate points of their "body." Or you can use a visual representation, such as a picture, or even a stuffed toy and perform the healing over this, connecting with their energy and acknowledging that you are using a visual representation.

Reiki is a fascinating form of healing; this is just a taste of what you can expect. You can incorporate crystals and other aids in your healing too. If you are really interested in reiki, then I recommend finding a reiki master to help take you through your training. However, if you just want to familiarise yourself with the basics and see if it is an energetic system that could work for you, then this should be enough to get you started.

Angelic Healing

Angelic healing is not a "method" of healing per se but is more focused on the energies we use. In a majority of the healing methods we have discussed, we are tapping into universal energy, prana, Qi, to perform the healing. However, in angelic healing the practitioner will channel the energy of the angels, letting them work through the practitioner to facilitate the necessary healing.

There are many different angels that can be called upon to deliver this healing energy. Below are just a few of the most popular ones and which areas in particular they are used in:

Angel Ariel—Ariel is the angel associated with nature and the environment, and she can assist us in connecting with the natural world. This includes animals, plants, nature spirits, and the elements.

Angel Azrael—Azrael is the angel of death and dying, aiding in transporting the souls of the dead to their resting place. In this sense, he is also known as the angel of comfort, as he can bring comfort to those who are grieving.

Angel Chamuel—Chamuel is associated with all aspects of love and relationships, and he especially useful for those who may be feeling as though love is lacking in their life, or who have difficulties expressing their love to others, or even perhaps express their emotions too easily.

Archangel Gabriel—Gabriel is associated with communication and creativity and can aid us in finding our voice and expressing ourselves. Gabriel is often depicted with musical instruments, such as the harp or the trumpet, or scrolls.

Angel Jophiel—Jophiel is associated with beauty, creativity, and inspiration. She can aid us in seeing the beauty in the world around us, which can aid us when we are feeling lost or hopeless.

Archangel Metatron—Metatron can be called upon to bring us balance in all areas of life. He is also associated with transformation and spiritual growth, and he is represented by the colour white.

Archangel Michael—Michael is associated with protection and courage. He can aid us in overcoming fear and negativity. He can also be called upon to help us release that which no longer serves us or we wish to be rid of. He is often depicted as carrying a sword and a shield, and the colour most often associated with him is blue.

Archangel Raphael—Raphael is associated with bringing general healing, whether that is energetic, emotional, or physical healing. He is also associated with relaxation and restoration. This angel is often depicted as carrying a staff or the caduceus, a common symbol of healing.

Archangel Uriel—Uriel is the angel of wisdom and enlightenment, and as such is often depicted with books and scrolls. He can aid us in uncovering the truth and bringing clarity when it is needed, and the colour red is often associated with him.

There is not a standard framework when it comes to angelic healing. Some practitioners will use crystals associated with angelic energies to perform the healing, whilst some may use Angelic Reiki. Angelic Reiki was "channelled" by Kevin Core through his work with Archangel Metatron between 2002 and 2003. It uses the core concepts of reiki (channelling energy into the chakras) but instead of connecting with a universal energy, you connect with the energy of the angels and use this in your healing.

You can seek out an angelic healing practitioner, or you can try connecting with these angelic energies yourself. I will admit, I am still on the fence as to how I feel about the concept of angels. However, I have always had surprisingly powerful results when working with angelic energies, so there is clearly something there that resonates with me. As such, I recommend giving this exercise a go even if you are unsure as to whether you believe in angels. You also may be pleasantly surprised at how effective this approach is for you in allowing you to tap into healing energies.

Connecting with Angelic Energies for Healing

First, set your intention. You may just wish to connect with general healing energies, or you may have a more specific healing you wish to perform, such as recovering from the hurts caused after an argument with a loved one. Once you have decided upon your intention, decide which angel is the most appropriate one to work with based on the list provided.

Find a quiet place where you won't be disturbed and sit or lie in a comfortable position. Close your eyes and shift into a meditative state. Mentally call upon your angel, and see yourself surrounded by a bright white light, and know this is the energy of your angel coming to aid you. Or maybe you even "see" that angel in your mind's eye, standing before you. The best thing to do is to keep an open mind, and let that angel send you healing in whichever way that they see fit.

Focus on your intent and ask your angel for guidance; you may even wish to state your intention out loud and ask them to send you this energy to help you heal. Feel that white light encompassing you, filled with the healing energy that you have requested. See it entering your body, flowing through your energy centres, and delivering that healing to where it is needed most. Listen for any messages that your angel may want to give you; as is usual with energy healing, these may not be spoken words, but images or symbols and the like.

When you are finished, thank the angel you have chosen to work with, and carry this energy with you, trusting that the healing is working.

Crystal Healing

In chapter 2, we used crystals to help us begin to sense energy. In this section, we will focus on using crystals specifically for healing yourself and others. They can also be incorporated into other methods of energy healing. For example, many reiki practitioners use crystals as a part of their healings to add extra energy to their work.

Crystals can be used for healing in a number of ways. You can hold them, as we did for the exercises in chapter 2, carry them with you, or wear them in jewellery. Or you can place them on, or hold them over, your chakras or areas of the body where you are experiencing issues so that they are closer to the source of the energy/issue you want them to heal. Here, we will be exploring crystal grids and how we can use the energy from these to aid us in our healing.

A crystal grid uses the same principles that we touched upon when we discussed combining the energy of different crystals in chapter 2. By combining these crystals and placing them in shapes based off sacred geometry, we can use these to facilitate a deeper level of healing.

Crystal Grids

To create a crystal grid, you will first need to decide what your intention is. Is it general healing, or is there a specific ailment, emotion, or such, you would like to heal? Are you looking to work with a specific chakra, or are you perhaps wanting to strengthen a particular colour in your aura? Once you have decided on your intention, you can choose crystals to include in your grid that match it.

Crystals can be expensive, and not all of us have the bank account to be able to spend money on five or six of the same crystal just in case we want to use it in a grid. If this is the case, you can also add other natural items into the grid to help supplement the power of any crystals you do use—shells, leaves, twigs, and other natural items all work well.

Once you have your items, you will need to decide how to place them. As I said, many people use sacred geometry to help determine the best shape, such as the flower of life. This needn't be complicated; for example, spirals spiralling outward represent banishing or removing something, and spirals spiralling inward represent drawing something toward you, such as healing. Circles represent completion and wholeness amongst other things and so are great for balance, peace, and healing. Below are some very basic shapes and their meanings for you to try with your own crystal grids:

Circles: Wholeness, completion, balance

Crosses: Protection, balance and equality (if using an equal-armed cross)

Diamonds: Connection with the higher self, intuition, and divinity

Spiralling Inward: Manifestation and drawing things toward you

Spiralling Outward: Banishing negative energies, habits, and generally sending things away from you

Squares: Building strong foundations, grounding, and establishing stability

Triangles: Creating opportunities

Advanced Sacred Geometry Shapes

There are more complex shapes that are used to form crystal grids. Here I have gone into a bit more detail on some of the most well-known ones, but this is by no means an exhaustive list. Whilst I always recommend the simplest options (which you are probably sick of me saying by now!), it can be fun, and extremely rewarding, to experiment with the more complex shapes for crystal grids.

Figure 15: The Flower of Life

The Flower of Life—The flower of life is an ancient symbol with different interpretations having been found in many different cultures for the past 6,000 years. One of the associations of the flower of life is creation. Within its pattern is the sacred knowledge of the universe, of time and space itself. Using it can aid us in understanding our place in that universe. Another association is that of life, connectedness, the cycles of birth, life, death, and rebirth, and the union of opposing energies. By working with the flower of life, we can achieve perfect balance within ourselves and unlock a higher state of consciousness.

There are several main shapes that comprise the flower of life, each with their own symbolism. You can work with each shape independently when forming your crystal grids, if you wish, rather than working with the flower of life in its complete form. Here is a brief overview as to the meanings of those symbolisms:

Vesica Piscis—First, we have the Vesica Piscis, which is formed of two circles overlapping each other, like a Venn diagram. This represents union and connectedness, the duality of all things. This is a good shape to use if you are feeling disconnected with yourself or the world around you, or if you feel that your energy is out of balance.

The Seed of Life—Next, we have the seed of life formation. It is formed of six overlapping circles surrounding a circle in the middle, so there are seven circles in total. Seven is a sacred number; there are the seven main chakras, seven colours in the rainbow, seven days in a week, and so forth. As its name suggests, it is associated with creation. It is a great shape to use if you are wanting to embark on a journey of transformation and to help release and move on from that which may be holding you back.

The Egg of Life—The egg of life consists of six circles that join around a central circle. The difference between this and the seed of life is that these circles don't overlap; they sit next to one another, and around the central circle. This geometrical shape is associated with new life and fertility. It is a good one to use if you are feeling stagnant and wish to reinvigorate your own energy and motivation.

The vesica piscis, the seed of life, and the egg of life all combine to form the flower of life, and it is this union of geometrical shapes that gives the flower of life its associations of creation, life, connectedness, and balance.

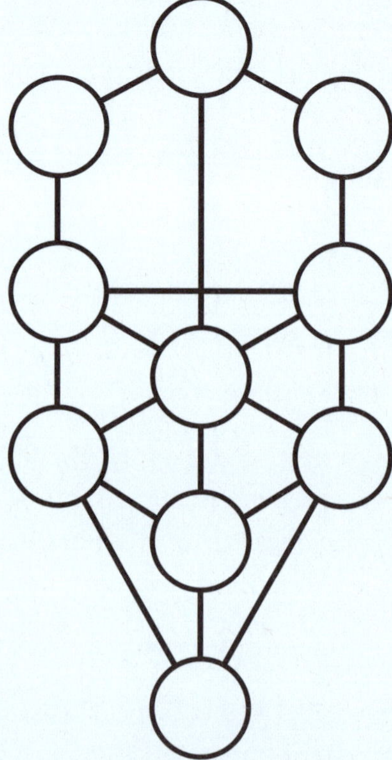

Figure 16: Tree of Life

Tree of Life—You may be familiar with the tree of life, as it has appeared in one form or another in various cultures and traditions from across the world. This symbol is a combination of straight lines and triangles, with ten different points along it. In the context of sacred geometry, it represents the structure of the universe, consciousness, the soul or higher self. It can also represent our journey through the various realms, which can be symbolic of our own personal journey through life. This is a great shape to use to help you connect to universal energy in general.

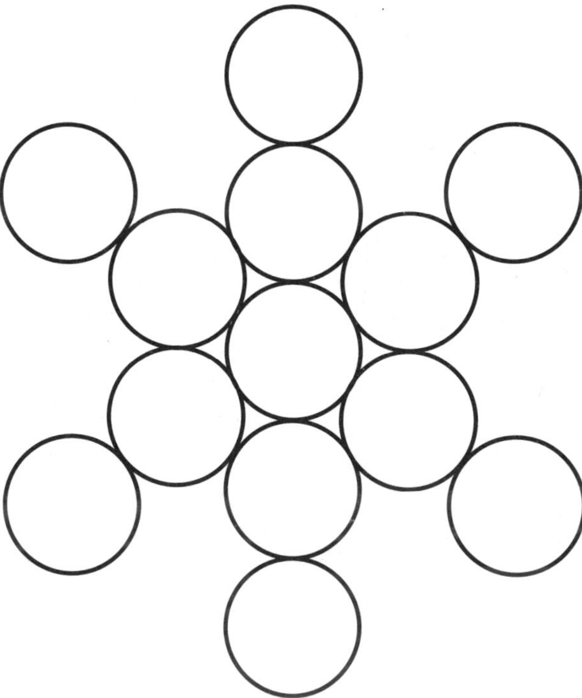

Figure 17: Fruit of Life

Fruit of Life—The fruit of life is made up of thirteen circles: five in a vertical line, and then four pairs of circles branching out from this central vertical line diagonally. Essentially, it looks a bit like a snowflake. Thirteen has long been considered a magical number, and the fruit of life represents unity and the connection between the other worlds and our physical realm. The fruit of life is actually present in the Flower of Life and Metatron's Cube (which we will discuss in more detail shortly), hence why I have split it out. I personally find that this is a good shape to use if you wish to send healing energy out into the world, by focusing on you (the healer) being in the centre, and then sending this energy out through the branches.

Figure 18: Metatron's Cube

Metatron's Grid/Cube—Metatron is an archangel and is known as the scribe of God. As the scribe of God, he would have recorded and known all secrets of the universe. It is said that this cube was created from the angel's own soul. It contains all the geometric shapes that exist in the world. As such, one of its associations is aiding us in connecting with divine energies. It again represents creation, balance, and harmony, and I personally find it a great shape to work with for energy healing and especially protection.

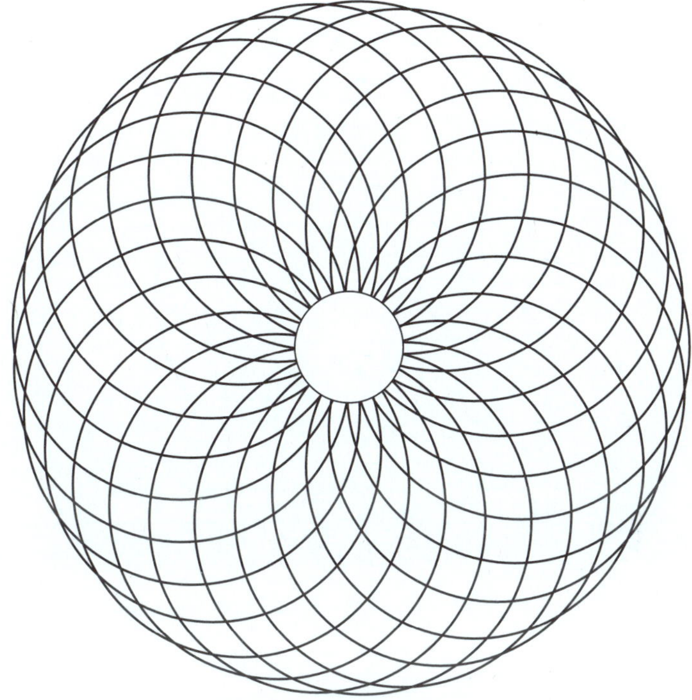

Figure 19: Torus

Torus—The Torus looks a bit like a vortex, with many overlapping circles connected to a central circle. It represents the flow of energy and the harmony that can be achieved when you are at one with your own energy flow and the energy flow of the universe. As such, it is a great one for energy practitioners to use to help them centre and connect with both their own energy and universal energy on a more spiritual level.

Figure 20: Merkabah Star

The Merkabah Star—The Merkabah Star is composed of two intersecting tetrahedrons that rotate in opposite directions (although of course this won't be visible if you are viewing the shape drawn on paper). It is associated with connecting with a higher power or higher realms. It represents duality and demonstrates the complexity in all things, bringing these into balance. It can be used to help us connect with our personal power, raise our own vibration, and also protect our energy like a force field.

Creating Your Grid

Once you have decided on your intention and the shape you will use to form your grid, you can move on to building it. You can buy crystal grids online; often they are wooden discs with one of the shapes above carved into it. I tend to go a bit DIY and print one off from online and stick it to a spare bit of cardboard. You also don't have to use any of these patterns if you don't want to! You may wish to try sketching out a design beforehand and then building from that, or you may wish to just listen to your intuition and place the items wherever it tells you to place them. Play around with it until you find the layout that works for you, and always keep your intention in mind as you are building your crystal grid.

Try to make sure that the crystals are all connected or joined to one another in some way. Quartz crystal points are excellent for this, as clear quartz is a natural conductor and amplifier of energy, but if you don't have any, you can use twigs or similar.

Once you have built your grid, you will need to activate it, and this can be done simply by stating your intent. For example, "I have created this grid for healing; may the healing energies of these crystals fill my heart and allow me to mend." Breathe this intention over the grid; remember, breath is energy and is great to use for such occasions.

You can then either meditate with your crystal grid using one of the methods in chapter 2 to absorb the energies of the crystal grid or you can leave it and allow the energies to permeate the room. This is especially useful if you have a dedicated healing space where you heal clients or even yourself.

Crystal Associations

It is good to know some of the most popular attributes and the crystals associated with them to help you get started on building your own grid. As with most of what I touch upon in this book, there is a wealth of information out there on crystals, so I won't go into too much detail, but this should give you an idea as to where to start.

Abundance: Green aventurine, goldstone, sun stone

Cleansing: Calcite, fluorite, clear quartz, selenite

Communication: Blue lace agate, angelite, kyanite, topaz

General Healing: Amber, amethyst, angelite, bloodstone, fluorite, malachite, moldavite, peridot, selenite, sugilite

Happiness: Aquamarine, carnelian, citrine

Love: Emerald, rose quartz, sugilite, ruby, moonstone

Peace: Amethyst, dolomite, kunzite, moonstone, strawberry quartz

Protection: Garnet, hematite, jade, jet, lapis lazuli, onyx, smoky quartz, tiger's eye, turquoise

Healing with Tree Energy

Trees and plants also contain their own energy, and you can interact with them in a similar way to how we do with crystals. The most powerful way to work with tree energy is directly, by meditating and working with the tree itself. However, I appreciate this isn't possible for everyone; I personally live in a big city where it can be difficult to find those green spaces with the needed tree. Even if there were, I know that I wouldn't be able to focus properly on connecting with the tree if there were a lot of people around, or even very few people around (from a personal safety point of view). As such, I personally tend to work more with twigs, leaves, and fruit from the corresponding tree.

I've always felt that there is something quite special about working directly with nature in energy healing. It's a pure energy, the very essence of this universal vibration, connecting us to the all. Going for a walk in nature is often recommended to boost our spirits when we are feeling low, and I believe that it is the energy that these natural elements emit that we subconsciously tap into and can elevate our mood.

When working with trees, it is important to ask for their permission first. I know this might sound silly, and also that I didn't mention asking for permission from crystals. This is just one of those things I have learnt through my own experience; tree energy can be quite sensitive, and to say that we as a species don't take as good a care as we should over our leafy friends is a bit of an understatement! Science has proven that trees can communicate to one another through their roots, and have a rich, interlinked existence. It is important to treat all trees with respect and reverence, whether you are just working with them once or wish to work with them on an on-going basis.

You can also use the Irish ogham to help connect with the energy of certain trees. In Irish mythology, this language was created by the god Ogma. It has existed in some form since the fourth century AD, although some believe it originated in the first century AD. It is often called "the tree alphabet," as many (but not all) of the symbols have been associated with trees, which were sacred to the Celtic Irish peoples. It is worth noting that there are many ogham lists—the tree ogham is just one of them.

The ogham alphabet originally consisted of twenty characters, with an additional five letters being added in later. *In Lebor Ogaim*, also known as *The Ogam Tracts* or *The Book of Ogams*, an old Irish treatise on the ogham alphabet, also introduces an additional ninety-two characters. However, for the purposes of divination, the original twenty-five are used. These twenty-five characters are split into five sections, (or "aicme")—first, second, third, fourth, and fifth.

In the following pages, I have included a very brief overview of just some of the ogham tree list. I find working with the Irish tree ogham symbols very helpful in connecting with the energy of a tree or plant, and for that reason I have also included the ogham name of each tree for you to easily find the associated symbol.

There are many ways you can incorporate tree energy into your own healing practice. For example, as well as working with the tree directly, or working with the leaf/fruit/twig, you can draw the corresponding ogham symbol on the area of your body associated with your healing intention.

Do remember that some trees and plants can be toxic or cause adverse effects if touched directly. Always make sure you do your research on a particular tree before interacting with it, and use professional advice to ensure that you have identified the tree or plant correctly.

The Trees and Their Ogham Symbols

The Fir Tree (Ailim)—Fir trees are evergreen trees with needlelike leaves, and there are many different species of fir. Their name is derived from the Latin "to rise," given the heights that they can grow to, which is fitting considering their healing potential. Working with the energy of the fir tree brings foresight and vision. It is useful to connect with when you may be experiencing energy blockages that are preventing you from seeing the way forward.

The Birch Tree (Beith)—The birch tree has a distinctive white bark, and it is associated with new beginnings, change, and letting go of the past. It can motivate us for the future, helping us get into the right frame of mind to accept these new beginnings and change. It is a great energy to work with to help you overcome energy blockages that may be caused by instances or situations that have occurred in your past.

Hawthorn (Huathe)—The Hawthorn tree has beautiful white flowers and pretty sharp thorns, and so it is fitting that this tree is associated with cleansing and purification. It can be used to help reinvigorate ourselves, almost like starting anew with a fresh slate. It brings patience so that we may mentally be in the right place to start moving forward. As such, the hawthorn is great to use if you wish to perform a general cleanse on your energy, or if you struggle with frustration or impulsiveness.

The Beech Tree (Phagos)—Interestingly, the beech tree is considered native in the south of England but non-native in the north. The energy of the beech tree brings wisdom and can aid us in connecting with inner knowledge. It is especially useful in helping us then apply this wisdom in our everyday lives, and so is a great energy to work with if you are struggling to find the confidence that you need to trust your judgment and decision-making.

The Poplar Tree (Eadha)—The poplar tree grows quickly but has a relatively short lifespan compared to other trees. This energy of the poplar is associated with victory and overcoming challenges and so can help us conquer our fears. It is a great tree to work with if you find yourself feeling anxious or stressed about life in general, or to help heal the blockages that prevent us from taking responsibility for our actions.

Heather (Ur)—Heather is one of my favourites; it has a beautiful energy. It is generally considered to be a shrub and not a tree, but it is too beneficial to not include. It can help us connect with the earth, experience a deep connection to energy in general, and guide us in connecting with our intuition. It is also associated with healing and so is a great one to use to help you connect more generally with healing energy. I personally keep a small glass jar with a corked lid with some dried heather (and moss, which is also associated with healing but not a part of the ogham) on my altar.

The Ash Tree (Nuin)—Whilst the heather represents connection to the earth, intuition, and energy, the ash tree represents connection with all things. It is often associated with the Norse World Tree, and so this can be other people, the world around you, or even yourself and your own thoughts, feelings, and purpose in life. As such, the ash tree is a great tree to work with to help you connect to universal energy, and it can help remove blockages caused by a lack of confidence or a lack of clarity.

The Oak Tree (Duir)—The oak tree is one of the most well-known trees, with more than 500 different species of oak. The energy of Duir is associated with opening doors and presenting us with opportunity. It can bring us strength and protection, and it is a great energy to work with to help resolve energy blockages that may prevent you from putting yourself out there or committing to or following through on your plans or ambitions.

The Spindle Tree (Oir)—The spindle tree is quite a small tree compared to the others in this list, but it is no less powerful! It aids us in ensuring we have the right mindset for manifestation, and it is a great tree to work to invigorate your energy, especially if you are taking on new ideas or new challenges.

The Hazel Tree (Coll)—The hazel tree has a very interesting relationship with fungi. There are several different species of fungus that have what is called a "mutualistic relationship" with the tree (meaning both the tree and the fungus benefit from this relationship), and it also provides nutrients to several rare species of lichen. The hazel tree has no problem sharing its resources and nurturing those around it, and so it may not be surprising to hear that the energy of the hazel tree is associated with the heart. It governs our emotions and how we feel and manage our feelings, our intuition, and can gently inspire us in all areas of life. As such, it is a great energy to work with where matters of the heart, or strong, emotional reactions are involved.

Ivy (Gort)—Technically ivy isn't a tree, but a plant. However, it is still listed in the ogham, and its energy is very useful in healing and so I wanted to include it. The ivy is associated with transformation and the mental faculties—memory, reasoning, perception. It is a good energy to use to help us dispel confusion and find the clarity we seek. It can be difficult to process and overcome negativity or situations that may have caused deeply rooted blockages, if we don't fully understand the how or the why of the situation. Ivy can aid us in being able to better understand the lessons of our lives so we can either integrate them into ourselves or move on from them.

The Willow Tree (Saille)—The energy of the willow tree is a very feminine energy, and as such it is associated with all things feminine, lunar rhythms and the moon, and our intuition. It has a very peaceful energy and can be a great one to use when you wish to calm and connect with your personal energy.

The Elder Tree (Ruis)—The elder tree is associated with birth and death. It can aid us in removing energy blockages by helping us to let go of that which no longer serves you, to say goodbye to one chapter in your life and start a new cycle.

Sound Healing

Have you ever listened to a song and it's changed your entire mood? Do you put on an upbeat playlist when you're exercising or listen to sad songs after a breakup to help you get the feelings out? Chances are you have been engaging in a form of energy healing without even realising it! It is well known that sound and music can have an impact on our mental and emotional selves, but it can also have an impact on our energetic selves.

Sound has long been used for healing. Remember in the chakra section we discussed the specific sounds associated with each chakra? That is a form of using sound to help empower and heal our chakras. This particular type of sound healing is known as vocal toning, which primarily uses vowel sounds to generate healing vibrations and energy.

Our bodies are made up of 75 percent water, and water is a great conductor of vibrations, especially the vibrations caused by sound. Certain sounds, and at certain frequencies or speeds, can create specific vibrations that can influence the vibrations of our own energy fields.

If you can, I highly recommend trying out a sound bath session. A sound bath is performed using singing bowls, gongs, or bells. If you can't get to a live session, there are some fantastic ones online you can listen to. Sound healing is one of my favourite types of healing, and I think in part that is because it is quite "passive"; you can lie there and let the energy do its thing without needing to focus so much on connecting with it or directing it. It is definitely my go-to when I am feeling too tired or out of sorts to do anything more "hands on," such as reiki or anything that involves visualisation!

The seven main chakras have specific frequencies associated with them, and you will find that most singing bowls are often attuned to one of these frequencies. As such, you can find a sound bowl that can be used specifically to help heal and empower the throat chakra (for example), as it resonates at the pitch associated with the throat chakra. This is why sound bowls tend to be of different sizes, adding an additional layer of healing into sound therapy. These are aligned to the Solfeggio frequencies.

Solfeggio Frequencies

The Solfeggio frequencies use specific sound patterns to affect our energy. It contains several frequencies formed out of sacred numbers—three, six, and nine—and each has a specific purpose. Even if you don't want to work with the chakras, these sounds can still help you heal blockages in your energy. The seven main frequencies and their associated chakras are:

396 Hz: Letting go of guilt and fear, grounding and stability (root chakra)

417 Hz: Helping you accept and pursue change, creativity and pleasure (sacral chakra)

528 Hz: Transformation and manifestation, building confidence (solar plexus chakra)

639 Hz: Relationships and connection (heart chakra)

741 Hz: Getting in touch with your intuition, communication and expression (throat chakra)

852 Hz: Getting in touch with your spirituality (third eye chakra)

963 Hz: Enlightenment and divine consciousness, peace and connection to universal energy (crown chakra)

Binaural Beats

You could also try binaural beats. Binaural beats are actually a perception of sound created by our brains. Using headphones, you listen to one tone with one specific frequency through one ear, and another tone with a different frequency through the other. The brain takes these and creates a third tone, and this is the binaural beat. There are some specifics when creating a binaural beat; the frequency of each tone in each ear needs to be less than 1000 Hz, and the difference between the two tones less than 35 Hz.

When listened to over a period of time, the beats can align with our own brainwaves and alter our brainwave activity. As I've mentioned before, our energetic selves are connected with our physical, mental, and emotional selves, so binaural beats can also be used to help influence our energy. Each frequency is associated with different levels of brain wave activity; here are just some of them:

Gamma Pattern—The highest frequency of brain activity between 30 Hz and 50 Hz. It is associated with concentration, memory, alertness, and can improve our mood.

Alpha Pattern—Ranges between 8 Hz and 13 Hz. It can help relax the mind and can even boost creativity.

Theta Pattern—Ranges between 4 Hz and 8 Hz, and it can be used to aid meditation.

Delta Pattern—The slowest brain waves. Ranges between 0.5 Hz and 4 Hz and can help bring restful sleep.

Planetary Energies

It is difficult to find someone who hasn't at least heard of astrology; the idea that the planets can affect our moods, emotions, energy, physical being, and our overall human experience. It is a theory that has prevailed through many different civilisations for thousands of years.

First off, for the purposes of this section I will be referring to the Sun and the Moon as "planets." I know they are not planets, but they still contain an energy that we can work with in our own healing, and so for ease of writing when I say "planets," I also mean to include the sun and the moon under this distinction.

It is unknown exactly when the classic planets were first "discovered." The Sun, the Moon, Mercury, Venus, Mars, Jupiter, and Saturn can all be seen with the naked eye, and records of them have been found throughout different cultures. The earliest record of Mercury and Saturn was most likely made by an Assyrian astronomer, and mention of Venus and Jupiter can be found in Babylonian texts. The earliest record we have of Mars comes from ancient Egypt. These bodies are known as the classical planets.

The only planets who we have definite discovery dates for are Uranus, which was discovered in 1781 by Sir William Herschal; Neptune, which was discovered by John Couch Adams in 1846; and Pluto, which was discovered in 1830 by Clyde Tombaugh.

These huge celestial bodies have their own energies that permeate throughout the universe. We can connect with and use these energies in our own workings.

Astrology is a huge subject, and there is too much information to be able to cover in one book. We will discuss each planet and their associations, and once I have gone through the celestial bodies and their energetic associations, I will be giving you some ideas as to how you can connect with these energies, so for each planet I will also list herbs/crystals/symbols associated with that body for you to incorporate once we get to this stage. First, let's look at magic squares.

Magic Squares

Magic squares have been around for thousands of years and through many different cultures although used in different ways and for different purposes. However, I want to focus specifically on the magic squares associated with the planetary bodies, and how we can use these to connect with the energy of these celestial bodies.

Whilst it is attested that magic squares associated with the planets have been written about for centuries, it is difficult to find credible sources to support this assertion. However, many people attribute the magic squares we most commonly associate with planets to Cornelius Agrippa, (full name Heinrich Cornelius Agrippa von Nettesheim), a German-born occult writer (amongst many other titles) who was born in 1486. As an occult writer, as he published the *Three Books of Occult Philosophy* in 1533.[12] His work on magic squares appears in the second of these books.

These squares are based on the planet's own planetary number. For example, the moon's planetary number is nine, so the moon's is a 9x9 square. The planetary number for Jupiter is four, so Jupiter's is a 4x4 square.

We can use the magic squares to create symbols, which draw on the power of the particular planet we want to work with to aid us in specific purposes.

First, think about the healing you wish to acquire; is it general healing or is there something more specific that you want to focus on? Once you have decided on your purpose, decide which planet best encapsulates the energy that you need.

Next, try to sum up your need as succinctly as possible. It may just be that one word will suffice, such as "health" or "peace." Or maybe you have a phrase or a need that is a bit more specific, such as "recovering from my breakup." You could shorten this to "recovering breakup."

Once you have determined this word or phrase, write it down. Some resources will recommend first erasing any repeating letters from your word or phrase; for example, if you were using the word *happiness*, erase the second *p* and *s* to leave you with "hapines." However, this isn't necessary; it can help create a "cleaner" symbol, and is especially useful if you have a phrase you are using rather than just one word, but as always, play around and see what works best for you.

Then, working with a key, you turn the letters into numbers, and you can now map them onto the appropriate planetary square to create your symbol.

12. Heinrich Cornelius Agrippa, *Three Books of Occult Philosophy by Heinrich Cornelius Agrippa*, trans. James Freake (Lost Book Project, 2024), Kindle.

1	2	3	4	5	6	7	8	9
A	B	C	D	E	F	G	H	I
J	K	L	M	N	O	P	Q	R
S	T	U	V	W	X	Y	Z	

Figure 21: Magic Square Key

Let's say I want to use this approach to create a symbol to help draw down the Moon's energy to bring me comfort, as I am feeling vulnerable after a bad day at work. I just have the one word rather than a phrase, which makes it easier—and there is just one repeating letter in the word *comfort*, which I am going to leave in as it is only a short word. Running it through my key, I would get the following:

C=3

O=6

M=4

F=6

O=6

R=9

T=2

I would then take a pencil and plot it onto the 9x9 square associated with the moon, starting with the box the number 3 is in, then drawing a line to the box that contains number 6, then through to 4, and so on until I have completed the word. You can then take it from the square, tidy it up a little bit, and thus you have created your own planetary symbol.

There are many ways you can then use the symbol you have created. You can draw it on your body, on a piece of paper, or even on a stone or a crystal and carry it around with you. You could sew it into your clothing or a bag or create a keyring to add to your keys. You could carve it into an appropriately coloured candle and burn it, you could carve it into a bar of soap and use it to wash yourself, bake the symbol into some cookies or a loaf of bread … the possibilities are endless, so use your imagination and get creative!

Planetary Associations

We will begin by taking a look at the individual planets and their basic associations. Many cultures and civilisations have assigned different meanings and different deities to the planets. For example, the Greeks and the Romans felt that the moon encapsulated very feminine energies and associated goddess with the Moon, but in Japan the deity associated with the Moon is male. I will be approaching this information from a Western viewpoint, drawing predominantly on Roman associations. However, if you are interested in working with celestial energies, then I recommend you look more in depth at other cultures and how they believed the energy of the planets governed the universe.

37	78	29	70	21	62	13	54	5
6	38	79	30	71	22	63	14	46
47	7	39	80	31	72	23	55	15
16	48	8	40	81	32	64	24	56
57	17	49	9	41	73	33	65	25
26	58	18	50	1	42	74	34	66
67	27	59	10	51	2	43	75	35
36	68	19	60	11	52	3	44	76
77	28	69	20	61	12	53	4	45

Figure 22: Square of the Moon

The Moon

The Moon is considered to have a very feminine energy. It is associated with femininity and goddess figures, and the qualities often associated with such, including nurturing, comfort, compassion, motherhood, and the element of water. It is also associated with mystery and all things that encompass it, such as dreams, prophecy, intuition, and the cycles of life.

The different phases of the Moon also carry different energies. The new moon is associated with new beginnings, and the waxing moon is associated with manifesting and drawing things toward you. The full moon is often considered the most powerful phase of the moon, so this is a great time to connect with moon energy to add extra "oomph" to your healing. The waning moon is associated with banishing and sending things away from you, whilst the dark moon is associated with shadow work, meditation, and introspection. I personally find the dark moon is a great time to focus on replenishing your own energy and work healing on yourself.

The Moon is associated with the day Monday, so if the Moon phase you need falls on a Monday, then even better.

The symbols associated with the Moon include the crescent moon, and also the triple moon (a full moon with two crescents connected to either side). Crystals associated with the Moon include moonstone, pearl, and selenite. If you wish to incorporate herbs, you could use poppy, iris, jasmine, mugwort, or evening primrose. For colour magic, silver, white, and blue are often associated with the Moon.

6	32	3	34	35	1
7	11	27	28	8	30
19	14	16	15	23	24
18	20	22	21	17	13
25	29	10	9	26	12
36	5	33	4	2	31

Figure 23: Square of the Sun

The Sun

The Sun is considered to have very masculine energy. It is associated with masculinity and god figures and the qualities often associated with such, including strength, confidence, vitality, authority, and leadership. It is also associated with wealth and abundance and a desire to be noticed or have the attention of others.

Again, like the Moon, the Sun has different phases that we can attune to in order to maximise the energy we require for our chosen purpose. Sunrise is associated with new beginnings, health, renewal, and finding the right direction. The morning is associated with growth, manifestation, happiness, and the expansion of ideas. High noon is associated with health and physical energy, whilst the afternoon is associated with business matters, communication, and clarity. Finally, sunset is associated with letting go and releasing, and it is a good period to focus on cleansing and ridding yourself of any negative energies you may have picked up during the day.

The day of the week associated with the Sun is, unsurprisingly, Sunday. The astrological symbol for the Sun is a circle with a dot in the middle of it. If you wish to incorporate crystals, then sunstone, goldstone, and pyrite are all great crystals to help you connect with this energy. If you are using herbs, try marigold, saffron, cloves, or juniper. The colours associated with the Sun are gold, red, orange, and yellow. Use spicy, warm scents such as cinnamon, saffron, cayenne, and ginger.

Now, I just want to note here that I personally feel uncomfortable with this traditional alignment of male and female roles. Strength is not just a masculine trait—women can be strong too. Just as nurturing isn't just a feminine trait, and men should be encouraged to be nurturing also. As a woman, if I'm looking to manifest strength, I will sometimes work with the Moon rather than the Sun in acknowledgment of this, so as always, do what feels right to you.

8	58	59	5	4	62	63	1
49	15	14	52	53	11	10	56
41	23	22	44	45	19	18	48
32	34	35	29	28	38	39	25
40	26	27	37	36	30	31	33
17	47	46	20	21	43	42	24
9	55	54	12	13	51	50	16
64	2	3	61	60	6	7	57

Figure 24: Square of Mercury

Mercury

Mercury is the planet of communication and travel. In the Roman mythos, the god Mercury was one of the most intelligent of the gods, so this planet is also associated with the mental faculties. He could be seen as a bit of a trickster god; as well as being associated with wealth, business, and good fortune, he was also known for his trickery and thievery.

Mercury is associated with Wednesday, and so this is a great day of the week to incorporate the energy of this planet. You can work with Mercury to help remove blockages that may be hindering your ability to communicate or to help with aspects associated with the mind such as letting go of painful memories or to bring clarity.

The astrological symbol for Mercury is the symbol for Venus, but with a half circle—like a crown—on top. You can also use the caduceus (a wand with two snakes wrapping themselves around it with two wings at the top). Crystals associated with Mercury include agate, jasper, and aventurine, and herbs include dill, fennel, mint, pine, and parsley. Bright greens and blues are the colours associated with Mercury.

11	24	7	20	3
4	12	25	8	16
17	5	13	21	9
10	18	1	14	22
23	6	19	2	15

Figure 25: Square of Mars

Mars

Mars is known as the planet of warfare and, like the Sun, is associated with masculine energies. It represents strength, force, action, saying no, and persistence, especially if the journey is long and hard or it is an activity we aren't exactly enthused about! The Romans saw Mars's military power and might as a path to securing peace rather than destruction. Mars can be described as stubborn, which is not always a bad thing. Mars energy can also help us be more impulsive and more confident in saying yes to opportunities when they arise.

The Roman god Mars was not only associated with war but also with agriculture, which I admit seems like an odd pairing. Mars energy is also useful for those green-fingered people who may want to tap into this energy to heal or help their plants flourish and grow. The energy of Mars is great for those who need to be more confident, and also for those who struggle to maintain boundaries or find themselves being taken advantage of.

Mars is associated with Tuesdays. The astrological symbol for Mars is the traditional "masculine" symbol, a circle with an arrow pointing up to the right which represents the shield and spear of the god. Crystals associated with this planet include bloodstone, red tourmaline, and red jasper. Herbs associated with Mars include gorse, thistle, tobacco, nettle, and dragon's blood. The colour associated with Mars is red.

22	47	16	41	10	35	4
5	23	48	17	42	11	29
30	6	24	49	18	36	12
13	31	7	25	43	19	37
38	14	32	1	26	44	20
21	39	8	33	2	27	45
46	15	40	9	34	3	28

Figure 26: Square of Venus

Venus

Venus is associated with feminine energies, and was often paired with Mars, creating a balance between masculine and feminine energies. This planet represents love, desire, romance, friendship, luxury, and opulence. Venus also represents beauty and all things associated with it—the arts, our physical looks and self-care, and generally the "finer" things in life. I personally find that this energy is great to work with when you are feeling a bit burned out and need to take the time out to focus on yourself and just indulge a little bit, something that is definitely beneficial in helping us preserve our own energy. Ridding ourselves of any blockages that are connected with our heart and our emotions can be aided by the energy of Venus.

The day of the week associated with Venus is Friday. As someone who works a traditional Monday to Friday routine, there is nothing I love more than connecting with this energy to unwind on a Friday evening after a long week at work, whether that's in helping me enjoy the company of friends with a few drinks at the pub, or curling up on the sofa with a huge bar of chocolate in my comfortable clothes and watching one of my comfort shows on TV.

The astrological symbol associated with Venus is the traditional feminine symbol of a circle with a cross beneath it. Crystals associated with Venus include rose quartz, calcite, chrysocolla, and tourmaline, whilst herbs associated with this planet include rose, lilac, ylang-ylang, jasmine, and willow. The colours most often associated with Venus are pink, pastel colours, and white.

4	14	15	1
9	7	6	12
5	11	10	8
16	2	3	13

Figure 27: Square of Jupiter

Jupiter

Jupiter is known for its benevolence. It represents stability, comfort, success, optimism, wealth, and justice.

Jupiter is also associated with expansion; often that is the expansion of ideas, of our own self-awareness and ideologies. It can also help us find a deeper significance within the world. As such, the energy of Jupiter is a good one to work with if you feel stuck, don't know how to progress, or wish to open yourself up to form a deeper connection with the world around you.

The Roman god Jupiter was the chief of all gods. He was associated with kings and rulership and teaches us not to hoard that which we have accumulated in our comfort, but to share it with others too. It is a great energy to work with if you experience energy blockages arising from selfishness, or if you tend to cut yourself off from others because you fear being taken advantage of.

The day of the week associated with Jupiter is Thursday. The astrological symbol for Jupiter looks like the number four but the left-hand straight line is actually a curve. Crystals associated with Jupiter include lepidolite, sugilite, and tiger's eye. If you are wanting to focus more on herbs then good ones to use include oak, wheat, barley, and horse chestnut (conkers). Use "earthy" scents, such as almond, walnut, liquorice. The colours associated with Jupiter are purple, royal blue, and gold.

4	9	2
3	5	7
8	1	6

Figure 28: Square of Saturn

Saturn

Many people have a negative view of Saturn in an energetic sense, but Saturn is a teacher. This energy can help us reflect on lessons learned through our experiences (both good and bad), learn from our mistakes, and tackle challenges head on and persevere through them. It teaches us commitment and responsibility where it might be tempting to bury our heads in the sand and face up to the difficulties we face; not just difficult situations but also bad habits and negative flaws we may possess within ourselves. It emphasises the need to tackle the root of our behaviours if we truly want to heal from them and turn our weaknesses into strengths. Saturn is a great energy to work with when you really want to look deep within yourself and tackle those energy blockages that may be deeply rooted or particularly painful, and will aid us in accepting them, learning, and moving on from them.

Saturn is associated with Saturday (again, unsurprisingly). The astrological symbol for Saturn looks like a lowercase *h*, with a line across the top of the letter, like the cross in the letter *t*. Crystals associated with Saturn are onyx, lodestone, apache tear, and black tourmaline. The herbs you could use to work with this energy include elm, ivy, wolfsbane, and yew. Scents such as sandalwood, cedar, frankincense, and juniper work well, whilst colours associated with Saturn include black, brown, and dark blue.

Neptune

Neptune is the planet of mystery and illusion. It is associated with our intuition and all spiritual matters. It is said that Neptune governs the unconscious mind and so can help us unearth our deepest fears and desires should we be brave enough to face them. Working with this planet can also help us understand the reality of a situation, rather than the reality we choose to see—are we fooling ourselves or being fooled by others? Neptune's energy can help us break through the illusions and see ourselves and what is happening around us for what it really is. This planet is a great one to work with if you struggle with blockages caused by all types of fears.

The Roman god Neptune was the king of the seas who had an unpredictable nature. He would send storms and earthquakes when in a temper.

The astrological symbol for Neptune looks like the head of a three-pronged trident, similar to the trident that the god was said to carry. Crystals associated with Neptune include lapis lazuli, turquoise, larimar, and aquamarine, whilst herbs and scents associated with this planet include orris, vanilla, lotus, valerian, myrrh, and mugwort. The colour associated with Neptune is blue.

Uranus

The energy of Uranus is a slightly rebellious one. It represents reform and radicalisation, change and transformation. This may be a deliberate change, or this may be a sudden or unexpected change. It is up to you to determine whether this change is a positive one or not. In these instances, Uranus can aid us in finding the positives and using it as a chance to transform ourselves and find a new way forward that we may not otherwise have pursued.

The planet is also associated with creativity and innovation and is a great energy to tap into when you need to shake things up. These could be changes in your external world, such as in finding a new career or a new purpose, or in your internal world, such as in making improvements to yourself or kicking bad habits. As such, it is a great planet to work with when you need to re-energize your own personal energy, or if you are embarking on a new path or journey.

The Roman god Uranus was a primordial sky god, but he was also a controversial figure who hid his own children away until their mother (Gaia) encouraged them to overthrow him.

The astrological symbol for Uranus looks like an uppercase *H* with a vertical line through the centre and a circle at the bottom of this line. Crystals associated with this planet include amazonite, angelite, clear quartz, and moldavite. Herbs associated with Uranus include fennel, lime, and allspice, and colour associated with it is a light blue.

Pluto

Poor Pluto has been demoted to the status of a "dwarf planet" in my lifetime, but I still consider it as influential as the major planets when it comes to its energetic impact. It is associated with the unseen, the unknown, and our shadow selves. This energy encourages us to explore the unknown, whether that is on a personal level or on a more philosophical, universal level. It aids us in looking past the obvious and helps us open our eyes and our understanding to that which we may not yet have seen or taken into account. In this sense, it also aids us in searching for those things we may have kept secret or hidden, even from ourselves, for us to work on.

Pluto is also associated with transformation, although this is often on a drastic level that involves the destruction of one thing to make way for the creation of something new. In Roman mythology, Pluto was the god of the underworld, which fits nicely with this planet's theme of secrecy and the shadow self.

The astrological symbol associated with Pluto is similar to the symbol for Venus, but the circle is instead just a half circle with a circle sitting within it. Crystals associated with Pluto include kunzite, smoky quartz, shungite, and black tourmaline, and herbs associated with this planet include wormwood, patchouli, dogwood, cedar, and cypress. The colours associated with Pluto include black and a deep red colour.

A Quick Note on Natal Charts

The moment that we are born onto this earth, the planets will be in a certain position in the universe. The position of these planets is mapped onto what is called our natal chart.

Within the natal chart you will find planets, signs, and houses. They all play a part in helping us understand our strengths, weaknesses, various personality traits, and where our energy is best directed or focused. To do this, we need to identify the planet, the sign (or constellation) it is in, and then the house it falls under.

We can use this knowledge to then better understand how the movements and positions of the planets affect our energy on a day-to-day basis as we navigate our lives. For example, my sun sign is Aries with a Cancer ascendant, which means I can be pretty emotional, take things personally, and feel the need to release these feelings quickly and abruptly when I have them! However, my moon being in Capricorn also means that whilst I may lash out over those small things, I struggle to open up to others about my emotions on a deeper level. Knowing this, I tend to practice cleansing probably more than the average healer. I also focus on journaling and shadow work to give me that emotional outlet, whilst working on healing to encourage me to feel more comfortable talking about my emotions with others.

There are plenty of websites that will build your natal chart for you, or you can pay an astrologer to build and interpret your chart for you. If you want to build your chart yourself, there are plenty of resources out there that will teach you how to do so.

You can still work with these planets and their energies even without understanding the specifics of your natal chart. However, if you are really wanting to go into the detail as to how the energy of the planets specifically affect you, then your natal chart is a good place to start.

You can also track the planets through the sky and how they interact with one another to gain an understanding as to how their combined energy could affect us. Again, there are plenty of online resources that will do this for you, but to give you an example; at the time of writing, the

Moon is in Libra. You may feel calmer, like you want to keep the peace, and feel more focused on creating harmony. Saturn is also in Pisces, and with Saturn being the planet of stability and comfort and Pisces being a sensitive water sign, these two are almost opposites. We may find that reality and fantasy can overlap, and we are unsure as to what it is we want and that our emotional wants might clash with our practical needs.

At the time of editing this book, Venus was in retrograde in Aries; with Aries being a planet associated with love and Aries's independence, I have heard friends saying that they know quite a few couples who have broken up during this period! If you are in a relationship, then questions as to whether your needs are being met in that relationship and whether you want to stay in it are bound to arise. Knowing to expect this can help you in managing those feelings in a healthier way than making rash decisions that you may regret later.

There is much more complexity with astrology than I am getting into here; it can depend on what direction the planets are travelling, how exactly they are aligning with one another, and such. But even this basic understanding will allow you to be able to understand and work with planetary energies on a deeper level.

For now, we will just focus on working with the planets themselves and the ways in which you can connect with their energy to aid you in your own healing.

How to Work with Planetary Energies

There are several ways you can connect to these energies. Remember, every tool you use is like a prop, a way to enhance your ability to connect to this energy. They aren't necessary, so don't feel put off if you don't have access to any of the below; even just meditation with nothing but your own energy will aid you in being able to connect to, and utilise, these energies.

Meditation—One of the ways I personally do this is to visualise myself in space, floating in front of the planet. Then I see my own energy expanding out and mingling with the energy of the planet, and then letting it fill me up.

Candles—Light a candle of the corresponding colour for the planetary energy you wish to work with and focus on that planet. You could even dress the candle with a scent associated with that planet to aid you or carve the symbol that represents that planet into the candle.

Symbols—You can create symbols using the magic squares that we discussed earlier for those planets that have them, or use the alchemical symbols associated with the planet you wish to work with. You can use these symbols in a myriad of different ways, again as listed in the section where I talk about magic squares in more depth, to help you carry the energy of the planet with you.

Create a Perfume—You can create a perfume using essential oils associated with the planet. You can spritz yourself with the perfume to again carry the energy of the planet around with you.

Create a Shrine—You could create a small shrine, either permanent or temporary, to the particular planet you want to work with. This is especially useful if you want to bring that energy into your home as well. It could include a picture or a model of the planet, candles, crystals, herbs and incense, or written poems dedicated to the planet in question.

Write a Prayer/Mantra—Reciting prayers or mantras can also help. These can be as simple or as complicated as you want. You can write a simple sentence, such as "I connect to the energy of Neptune," or something several verses long. So long as you can memorise it and it helps you attune to that energy, then it will work.

Learn about the Planet—Visit an observatory or do some research online or in a library to learn and understand more about the planet. Understanding its composition and history will help strengthen your connection.

Healing with Natural Spirits

I debated including this section in the book, as I was not sure if it was entirely in keeping with everything we have discussed so far. However, as someone who does personally work with nature spirits and has used them in healing, I thought that was reason enough to include it. It may be that you personally don't believe in spirits or have absolutely no desire to work with them if you do. If this isn't something you believe is relevant to you and your beliefs or the way you work, then that's okay! As with everything in this book, my main goal is to help you find ways of working with energy that resonate with you, and through which you can build your own ways of working. However, if nature spirits are an area that interests you, then I hope you find something worth pursuing in this section.

I have deliberately referred to the beings we will be discussing as "natural spirits" rather than "spirits." This is because when we talk of spirits, most people think of the spirits of the dead, or ghosts. I personally do not work healing with such spirits and so, for the purposes of this book, this is not a subject I will be touching. However, I do work with land spirits and animal spirits in my healing, and so we will be focusing specifically on these and how we can use their energies in our workings.

Exactly what natural spirits are is a matter of great debate. As with a lot of things that touch the metaphysical, there is not one agreed upon definition. I personally believe that these are beings that tread the path between this physical plane and the "other planes"; I personally refer to it as the "otherworld," or occasionally the astral plane. There are many different natural spirits known to have healing abilities, and so the following will by no means be a complete list of all of them.

Working with natural spirits can be a controversial topic. Some people do not feel comfortable doing so, and for good reason. Not all natural spirits are "light and love." They can have their own personalities and motivations, and not all of them are positive, just like people. There are occasions where a spirit may not be what they seem, perhaps masquerading as a benevolent spirit in order to hide their true intentions. However, the ones I have listed are ones that I have worked with myself and have never had a negative experience with. If you do decide to work with natural spirits, I recommend making sure that you do your research, and are well practised in protection, just as a precaution.

It is worth spending the time to build a relationship with any natural spirit you wish to work with. They are sentient and aware beings with their own thoughts, motivations, and desires. I'm sure we have all had that one friend who conveniently forgets their wallet whenever you go out for dinner or expects you to drive them everywhere; but the minute you need a favour, they disappear. Over time, it can make us very reluctant to help them. This is in the same vein as we should approach building a relationship with a natural spirit we wish to call upon to aid us in our healing. If you are constantly taking but never giving anything in return, they won't want to work with us for very long.

Leaving small, regular offerings for any natural spirits you wish to work with is a great way to help build that relationship so that they may be inclined to help you when you need it. For example, you could dedicate a candle or incense to them and burn it. Or you could collect litter in your local area and dedicate that act to them.

There are many ways in which you can work with these natural spirits to aid you in your energy healing. In general, I have found that the majority of these natural spirits are best suited to call upon when you wish to heal the local environment, rather than the self or others. However, there are a couple of exceptions, which you will see in this section.

You may wish to meditate and call on them to fill you with healing energy or visualise them sending this energy to you or the land around you. Or you may wish to call on them and ask them to grant you the energy to use in your healing, similar to calling the angels in angel healing. You could create a charm or similar and ask them to imbue it with healing energy, or simply utter a prayer to them. Working with natural spirits does not have to be complicated. In fact, the most difficult part is building and maintaining that relationship with them as opposed to actually working with them.

Creating Healing Water

One of my personal favourite ways is to ask a natural spirit to imbue water with healing energy, which I will then use to water my plants or pour onto the land to bring healing to that particular place. Below is my own personal method of creating "healing water" that can then be used in any way you see fit.

You will need:

- A bowl of water. Spring water is ideal but tap water will do. Similarly, any bowl will do, but my favourite is a small bowl made of quartz, as quartz is a great crystal to amplify energies. As this bowl is made of crystal, I never use it to consume any of the water; this water is only for pouring out onto the land and my plants.
- Incense
- A bottle to store the water in if you aren't going to use it immediately. Glass is preferred, as plastics can leach into the water over time.

Find a quiet space where you won't be disturbed and lay out your items. Clear your mind and focus on the spirit you would like to work with and your intent—to ask for healing energies. I often work with the Sisters of Avalon when creating healing water, so you will notice that this chant has nine verses to represent the nine sisters. However, this chant is relevant no matter which natural spirit(s) you call upon.

Take the incense in your hand and dedicate it to your chosen natural spirit before lighting it. You may say something along the lines of:

"I dedicate this incense to the Sisters of Avalon. I pray that you will accept it as an offering of the love I hold for you, and that you will bless this water with your healing power."

Once you have lit the incense, turn your attention to the bowl of water. Visualise it shining with a bright, white, healing light—healing that has been gifted by the spirit you are working with. Using the index finger on your dominant hand, stir the water clockwise nine times (make sure your hands are clean! Or you could use a spoon or similar object if you would prefer), stirring once for each of the verses below as you recite them out loud:

"Power of the [natural spirit name], shining bright, I invoke your healing this sacred night.
Water calm and water pure, blessed to heal, and heal to cure.
Sea and river, lake and rain, to heal all ailments, relieve all pain.
Spirits come, true and fair, bless these waters, heed my prayer.
I heal the sick, the plagued, the weak, for those that need this water seek.
Healing comes, this water blessed, harken to my one request.
Peace and health in body and mind, all malady is left behind.
Remove all that which harms the soul, and leave what needs it pure and whole.
Nine times this blessing cast on thee, and so I will it, mote it be."

Continue to visualise the water shining with this healing light, blessed by the power of your spirit, until you feel the ritual has been completed. Then thank your chosen natural spirit(s) for working with you, bottle the water (if you are not using it immediately), and let the incense burn down.

Natural Spirits of Healing

The following is a list of spirits you could work with. Each of these spirits has an association with healing, whether that is healing the land or healing the self. They are generally safe to work with and are ones I tend to work with regularly. Of course, this does not encompass every natural spirit out there who has an affinity with healing. As always, this information should serve as a good starting point to branch out and do more research if this is a subject that interests you.

The Well Maidens—The Well Maidens are natural spirits that appear in Arthurian legend. They actually only appear in one tale: the Elucidation. Believed to have been written in the early thirteenth century, it existed in a single French manuscript and has proven difficult to translate. To summarise, the Well Maidens were "keepers of the wells." A traveller only needed to stop at one of these wells and they would be greeted by one of the maidens, who would provide them with any drink or food they wished until they were ready to continue on their journey. However, one day the king at the time abused their hospitality, and the Well Maidens disappeared. The land slipped into decline and became a wasteland, and so Arthur and his Knights embarked on a mission to find the Well Maidens, bring them back, and restore the land.

Through this tale we can see that the Well Maidens are intrinsically tied to the land, and so they are great natural spirits to call upon to help bring healing energies to gardens or forests. I have also found that they are great in aiding us in healing ourselves, specifically any emotional hurts we may be feeling. If you have a natural well near you, it is a great place to go and connect with the energy of the Well Maidens. Unfortunately though, these are few and far between in this day and age. I have found that meditation is a great way to connect with the energy of these spirits and ask for their assistance in healing.

The Sisters of Avalon—This is another set of natural spirits from Arthurian legend. Avalon was said to be a magical island ruled by nine sisters who were said to be especially skilled in healing. They were led by their chief sister Morgen (it is believed that this character may have later become the renowned Morgan le Fay), who was said to be the most skilled of them all. It was here that Arthur was bought for healing after he was mortally wounded. I have found that these natural spirits are great to work with to learn more about healing; through meditation and journeying, they have presented me with specific symbols and such that I have used in my own healing practice.

Nymphs—In Ancient Greek mythology, nymphs were nature spirits that often took the guise of beautiful women. They were loved by gods and mortals alike and were often worshipped very similarly to gods by the Greeks. There were different classifications of nymph depending on the location:

- **Dryads:** Associated with trees, especially the oak tree
- **Naiads:** Associated with fresh water, such as rivers, springs, and lakes
- **Nereids:** Associated with salt water, such as the sea and the oceans
- **Oreads:** Associated with mountains

It is worth noting that there are stories of nymphs punishing those who disrespect them and their environment, so make sure you always approach them with respect (as you should any nature spirit!). In Ancient Greece, there is evidence of natural grottos being dedicated to nymphs, and later artificial ones being built and filled with plants, flowers, and fountains, and so tending an area of nature associated with them is a great way to bring healing to the local environment and ask for their blessings.[13]

Deities/Spirits of the Springs—Natural springs were very often associated with healing, and there is an abundance of tales of spirits and deities that were associated with springs and healings. One of the most well-known here in the United Kingdom is Sulis,

13. *Britannica*, "Nymphaeum," accessed March 31, 2025, https://www.britannica.com/art/nymphaeum.

a goddess of the healing springs in the city of Bath. In fact, you can still visit her temple in Bath, and there is a spa nearby that is fed by the same waters as the spring. I have visited it once before and found it a very powerful experience, and one which I would recommend to anybody who gets the opportunity.

Another is Coventina, a Romano-British goddess whose well resides at Carrabruff, who is often depicted as a water spirit who is partially clothed and reclining on the water or on top of water lilies. Then there is the god Grannus, who is associated with "Aquae Granni," now Aachan in Germany, a town that has its own thermal springs; Segata, a goddess whose healing spring was located in La Riviere, France; and Glanis, a god who was associated with the healing spring in the town of Glanum in the mountains of Southern France.

All these nature spirits and deities can be called upon to aid you in your own healing. It is ideal if you have access to a spring, but again these can be hard to come by, and is it not an absolute necessity to be able to work with these beings.

Animal Guides—We can also work with the energy of certain animals to aid us in all manner of things, including healing. You do not need to be in the physical presence of the animal (and in some cases, it is probably best not to be!). However, you can use meditation or journeying to help connect with that animal and its energy in your healing practices. Or maybe you wish to use a physical representation of the animal, such as a dog collar, if you wish to work with the energy of the dog to aid you. Here are just some of the animals often associated with healing:

Bears
Deer
Dogs
Frogs/Toads
Snakes

Swans
Whales

Practising Energy Healing on Others

Being able to connect to energy and use it to heal ourselves is a gift. Once we start to see our successes and realise the positive effects it has on our lives, it is natural that we would want to share it with others and use it to help heal those around us. Whether this is through reiki, EFT tapping, or crystal therapy, you can use any of the methods in this book to help heal others. This isn't just limited to other people; animals, trees, and plants can also benefit from the healing energy you can send them.

Whilst you can apply any of the healing methods in this book to healing other people, there are some additional elements you will need to consider before you start practising healing on others.

Energy Management and Consent

One of the obvious differences is that you are focusing on sending energy—whether in person or long distance—to another, rather than taking it into yourself. We are now acting as "the middleman," a conduit through which this universal energy can be harnessed and directed into another.

As we said in the "preparing for energy healing" section, most methods require you to connect with an external energy source rather than using your own energy. This is for your own benefit as well as that of your client; not only can using your own energy leave you feeling drained but there is also a chance that you could subconsciously take on any negative energies the client is feeling. You may also risk transferring any negative energies you may be harbouring to the client (even deep-rooted ones that you may not be aware of).

Make sure that you have put the practice in and feel confident in being able to use universal healing as opposed to your own energy, and that you can channel this into another appropriately. When I first began along this journey, I had a large poppet that I practised with in place of a real person or animal. You can always use a natural object, such as a stone or a twig, to act as your "client," and practice sending healing energy into these.

It is important to always make sure you get permission from your client if you are working healing on another person. You may wonder why this is necessary. We talked about the ethical considerations of energy healing in chapter 1, and I did say that there was no wrong or right answer. It is dependent on your personal moral compass.

However, as I touched upon in that ethics section, I have learned through experience that sending energy healing to those who are unaware of your intention does not usually work. If you have ever had any form of energy healing performed on yourself, you will know that it is something you can really feel; the more adept the healer, the more strongly you can feel the energy flowing through your body. To those who are not expecting it, or for those who aren't attuned to energy in the same way as I'm sure you are, this can be an alien experience. They may have never felt such energy before, and it can be a very uncomfortable experience. It may make them feel jittery or anxious. Even for those who are more attuned to energy, this unexpected surge of energy can feel uncomfortable. These people will often subconsciously "deny" this energy, or even actively reject it. So not only could your attempts have the opposite effect of your intention—by making them feel out of sorts rather than calmed and healed—but your efforts will also most likely be wasted. So, for your sake, as well as the sake of the person you are wanting to heal, it is always best to get their permission and make sure they are prepared to accept the healing before you proceed.

In-Person Healing Versus Distance Healing

You need to determine whether this will be long-distance healing or in-person healing, and if it will be in person, then will it be hands on or hands off? Long-distance healing is just as effective as in-person healing—don't think that you need to be physically present for healing to work! I personally prefer long-distance healing, as it allows me to help more people.

If you are performing healing in person, you can either touch them directly where appropriate or simply keep your hands a few inches above their body. Many practitioners perform the hands-off method, as it is generally more comfortable for both them and the client. If you do want to perform a hands-on healing, then you must take the necessary precautions. Ensure that your client is comfortable with this approach and explicitly agrees to it, make sure your hands are clean and warm, and give them a detailed rundown as to the areas you will be placing your hands, when, for how long, and so on.

In-person healing can be easier because you have the energy of the person "physically" there in front of you, which you don't when performing long-distance healing. This makes it much easier to connect with, to be able to diagnose any blockages, and then perform the healing.

If you are performing a distance healing, it is still important to connect with energy of your client, but you will need to do so in different ways. This could be a video call, through a picture of them, or even just email/online messages/text apps. I personally prefer to have a short online chat with whoever I am performing the healing on, asking questions such as how they are feeling, what they have been up to, or if there is anything in particular they would like me to focus on. You can tell a lot about a person by the way they communicate, and this can be a great way to help connect with them in an energetic sense.

Before you start the healing, make sure you have performed the steps in the "preparing for a healing" section. Both you and your client should be comfortable, and you should have performed the necessary cleansing and protection exercises on yourself before you connect to the energy and perform the body scanning technique on your client. When performing this long distance, I find it is useful to visualise the person's energetic self sitting in front of me. I usually see this as a distinct outline of them, fuzzy and blurry, made up of lots of tiny particles of energy buzzing away rather than a physical form.

If you find that visualisation doesn't do it for you, then you may wish to use a physical aid for this and the healing in general. You could use a large stuffed teddy or poppet and visualise it as your client lying before you. You could write their name on a piece of paper and place it on the aide to help you, or use a photo of them, and use these as a focal point through which to send the energy.

Once you have completed your preparations, perform your healing using your chosen method.

Finishing a Healing

Once you have finished, there are also a few closing steps you should perform. First, perform a quick grounding on yourself to rid yourself of any excess energies. I usually use a combination of the roots meditation method I explained earlier in the book and the Qi Gong movement "Pulling Down the Sky" to "push" the energy down through my roots.

Next, remember that, as with all healing, it can take a little time to recover. Advise your client (or yourself) to stay hydrated and to take it slow for the next couple of hours, or until they feel ready. Finally, you will want to perform another cleansing on yourself to rid yourself of any energetic connections to your client you may have created, or any negative energies you may have picked up from the client as you were performing the healing.

Other Useful Tools for Energy Healing

One of the great aspects of energy work is that it requires very little in the way of tools. All you need is you and the will to work to build your connection both with your own internal energy and the universal energy that surrounds us. However, tools can be beneficial for a variety of reasons. They can help empower our workings, provide a focus for us to better make this connection, and help us feel more confident in our practice. There is nothing wrong with using tools so long as you aren't expecting the tool to do all of the work.

So, what could you expect to find in the energy workers toolkit? Below are some of the tools of the trade you may come across and how you could use them to support your practice. I've only included those I haven't mentioned so far; crystals, incense, and such are often staples of a healer's toolkit, but I don't touch on them in this section. Remember, these are here simply to enhance your energy healing practice and your connection to energy and will still need your input to aid in successful healing.

The Pendulum

Pendulums can be used to aid you in understanding the flow of energy. Dowsing with either dowsing rods or a pendulum is a popular way of searching for ley lines or other areas where there may be an increase in energetic activity. The pendulum can also be used to help identify where there may be energy blockages within yourself or a client.

I have always used a pendulum rather than dowsing rods, so I will only be giving instructions on using the pendulum in this section. Anything can be used as a pendulum so long as it has enough weight to be able to swing. If you take a trip to your local metaphysical shop or look online, you will see pendulums of all different shapes and made from all sorts of materials.

Your main concern when choosing a pendulum is to choose one you feel drawn to, rather than searching for a specific colour or material. I have worked with pendulums that looked pretty but I just could not connect with on an energetic level and so were effectively useless. My current one is made from Amazonite crystal that I picked up at a local fair; I very rarely buy anything these days (after more than twenty years of practice I've amassed more than enough!) but I was immediately drawn to this one. I decided to leave it and continue looking in case I found something else I liked, but I could not get it out of my head—I was drawn to it. So far, it has served me much better than many of the other pendulums I've tried.

Spend a few minutes connecting with your pendulum and observing how it swings. Most pendulums will have a "preferred" way of swinging, whether that is in a circular motion either clockwise or counterclockwise, back and forth, left to right. Areas of increased energetic activity or blockages can be identified by the pendulum swinging in a completely different way to its usual swing, or it may retain its usual swing but swing faster or more pronounced.

Once you understand how your pendulum swings, slowly walk around the area you are present in if you are searching for ley lines and the like (more on ley lines later). If you are using it to help uncover energy blockages in yourself or another, move the crystal slowly up and down the body, paying attention to its swing. If it begins to exhibit unusual or erratic behaviour, chances are you may have found something. You can then use this knowledge to help you determine the best course of action if you encounter any blockages.

If you are using your pendulum for energy work, then I recommend you cleanse it regularly to help rid it of negative energies. You can use any of the cleansing methods listed in chapter 2, but instead of performing them on yourself, perform them on your pendulum. For example, you could pass it through the smoke of incense (smoke cleansing), use sound to cleanse it, or hold it under running water (a tap will do as opposed to a shower) to remove any negative energies.

Divination

Divination is not used as a tool to actively aid us in healing but, similar to the pendulum, it can help us identify blockages and give insight as to the best way to proceed with any healing we may be considering.

There are many types of divination, and each can be used to facilitate in healing. For example, one of my favourite forms of divination is lithomancy. Using the foundational principles of lithomancy, I created my own set which, when cast, will give an insight into where blockages within the chakras may be and give guidance on how to unblock them. You could use tarot cards and oracle cards in a similar fashion; by asking questions you could uncover sources of negative energy, or blockages, that you may have been previously unaware of. Questions you could ask to aid you include:

"Where is the negative energy I feel around me manifesting from?"

"What actions can I take to unblock my solar plexus chakra?"

"Where in my life am I currently experiencing energy blockages?"

"What actions should I take to better improve my energetic health?"

"What effect will performing this healing have on me in the long term?"

To give an example, I asked my tarot cards the first question in the list: where is the negative energy I feel around me manifesting from? I drew the Three of Pentacles reversed, the Page of Cups, and the Hermit.

The Three of Pentacles reversed signifies that there is missing collaboration and a lack of teamwork. One of the associations of the Page of Cups is being open to new ideas and unexpected surprise, whilst the Hermit represents a period of self-isolation. I would interpret this as signifying that this negativity is coming from my own isolation; I have been shutting myself away and not engaging with others, which is having a detrimental impact. The Page of Cups was interesting; at the time I did this reading, I was at a point in my life where I was feeling restless and bored. I had felt like I had achieved all of my main goals in life—I owned my own property, had a book published, had a good job—and felt like I had nothing left to achieve or throw myself into. Therefore, to me, the Page of Cups represented making sure that I was open to anything new, to put myself out there and say yes to whatever came my way (which relates well to the self-isolation aspect of the reading).

From here, I could look at different energy healing methods and determine which ones would be best for me. As someone who works a lot with the chakras, I decided that I should work on opening my heart chakra and my sacral chakra to encourage me to get out there, be more sociable, and be open to new ideas. Or perhaps I could create a crystal grid using sacred geometry and specific crystals, or I could work with the energy of the oak tree and the ash tree to achieve the same effect.

If you believe that someone may be directing negative energy at you, scrying or dream interpretation can be good approaches to understanding who may be sending that negativity your way. You may not "see" the exact person, but you could be presented with signs and other clues as to who may be wishing harm upon you.

Power Crystals

Some practitioners will work with what they call a "power crystal" (or a term similar to it). Whilst crystals are very beneficial to energy healing, and we will often choose certain crystals depending on the specifics of the healing we are performing, the power crystal works in a different way.

The power crystal is one crystal that the practitioner feels an affinity with, a deeper connection. They use this to enhance their connection with universal energy and bring extra power to their workings. This connection with the crystal is built up through constant use, thus empowering the crystal and creating a personal link with it.

I have a thick clear quartz point that I have owned since I was a young teenager and I wear in a necklace. I received it as a free gift from a copy of a *Mind, Body, Spirit* magazine that was in circulation many years ago now. As one of the first crystals I owned, it was instantly special to me, and over all these years (and with all of the crystals I have owned) it is still special to me.

Whilst clear quartz is a great choice, as its main association is amplifying energy and allowing us to better connect to it, your power crystal can be any crystal that you feel drawn to, for whatever reason. Once you have found your crystal, connect with it and nurture that connection. Cleanse it regularly, meditate with it, and charge it in the moonlight (or sunlight, depending on the crystal). Carry it with you to help it attune to your energy, and yours to it; you may wish to wear it in jewellery, carry it in your pocket, or sleep with it under your pillow. Most importantly, incorporate it into your energy practice wherever you can. This could just mean meditating with it, wearing it when you are practising creating energy orbs, or keeping it near you as you perform energy healing. The more you use it, the more attuned and connected you will become with it, and thus more connected to your own internal energy and the universal energy that surrounds us.

Poppets

A poppet is a doll that is made to represent a person and can be a useful aid in healing yourself and others. These dolls are often quite simple in their design, with legs, arms, a torso, and head, and often made from felt or material that is easy to sew. You can either buy them premade or make one yourself. I always recommend making them yourself, as it helps strengthen the connection you have to it. A poppet can be made for a one-off working, or it can be one you work with long term.

Poppets are often stuffed and dressed with items that reflect the intention it has been created for, so it is important to determine its use before you get started. You could create a poppet to represent yourself, but they are most commonly used to represent others. They provide a link between us and the person we are working with, which is especially beneficial when we are performing distance healing. It personally doesn't make much sense to me to create a poppet of yourself or someone you have physically around you and you can focus the healing on, but again this is just my opinion. You may feel completely different, so if you want to create a poppet that represents you and work with that, then give it a go.

How to Make a Poppet

The most important thing we need to do is create that energetic link between the poppet and the person you are healing. This is most commonly done by including something owned by the person in the poppet. This could be their hair, an object of theirs you have been gifted, or a letter with their handwriting, for example. These things can be difficult to come by, so if you aren't able to source an object they have personally interacted with, then a photograph of them, or even their name and date of birth written on a piece of paper will do.

To create your poppet, you will need:

- Fabric
- Fabric marker (or writing tool to outline poppet on fabric)
- Scissors
- A needle and thread
- Some stuffing (even an old T-shirt or holey socks cut into pieces will do in a pinch)
- The items you wish to include in it.

Start by drawing the outline of your doll onto the fabric (remember that you will need a back and a front), cut these out, and start sewing them together around the edges. Make sure you leave a space to stuff your doll. Do not worry if the legs are too short, or the sewing is messy; it is your intention that matters the most.

Once you have completed this step, it is time to stuff it. You will need to include the item that will create the link between the poppet and the person it represents at the very least. Otherwise, you could include crystals, herbs, drops of oil, charms, and any other items you can think of so long as they are associated with your intent and won't go bad or spoil (such as food items).

Let's say for example that I am performing a distance healing on one of my close friends. I perform the body scanning technique outlined in the "preparing for healing" part of chapter 3 and determine that they have a blockage in their root chakra. In this instance, I would leave a gap to stuff the poppet near the base of the spine, the area associated with the root chakra. I would then place a piece of paper with their name and date of birth in this area first. I could then place a small pebble, to represent the element of earth that is associated with grounding; a piece of red jasper, as red is the colour associated with the root chakra; and a few drops of cedarwood oil, a scent also associated with the root chakra. I would then sew my poppet up.

Let's say that my friend is having to deal with extremely toxic people in their place of work. In this instance, I would include the piece of paper with their name and date of birth in the poppet again, but also a piece of onyx for protection, an acorn for strength, a couple of pinches of dried chamomile to bring peace, and a couple of pinches of dried heather to promote general healing.

Once you have stuffed your poppet, finish sewing it up. You may wish to add more features to it; for example, you could sew on some buttons to represent eyes, draw on a mouth, or even give it clothing. You may wish to draw the main meridians and energetic pathways onto the poppet, or mark the main chakras with a pen in the colour associated with that chakra.

You will then need to enchant your poppet, effectively bringing it to life and activating it. First, hold the doll and focus on the person it is representing, and when you feel ready, say: "I name you [person's name], so that you may be connected to them and deliver [intention] to them."

Then breathe on the doll three times. Remember that our breath is sacred energy, and so it will breathe life into your doll.

From here, you can either keep your doll in a safe place until it is no longer needed or you can continue working with it. You could use it to perform other healing on it, such as reiki to send healing energy to the person it represents, or you could chant mantras over it or anoint it with oil that corresponds to the healing you wish to send. Remember that it is a physical representation of the person you are sending healing to, so treat it as well as you would treat them—don't just throw it in a dark box beneath your bed and forget about it!

Once there is no longer a need for your poppet, you can dispose of it, but first you need to sever the link between it and the person it represents. To do this, sprinkle salt over the poppet whilst visualising a cord connecting them and that person, and that cord being broken with harm to none. Make sure you do this with the utmost respect, thanking the poppet for its service as you do so. Finish by chanting:

"I thank you, poppet, for your service,
And for your aid in [intention].
I now break the cord between you and [person].
No longer are you connected but separate."

Ring a bell or chime a gong or singing bowl three times over the doll to signify an end to this process. Many people recommend burying the doll in earth, but I personally prefer to completely disassemble it, discarding any items that can't be reused (such as the material, thread, any paper bits, etc.), and cleansing anything that can be (such as crystals) to be used again in the future.

Rather than creating a poppet for each person you heal, you may wish to create one poppet and use that with every client (this is personally my preferred approach if I choose to use poppets). Just make sure that you cleanse the poppet after each use to ensure that the energetic link is broken before you use it with your next client. I often use incense to perform a smoke cleanse to achieve this, but any of the cleansing methods listed in chapter 3 will work.

Chapter Four Reflections

We have covered a lot in this chapter, so there are also more exercises here than you will find in the rest of the book. These reflections will help point you in a direction (I won't say "the right direction," as what is right for me may not be right for you), as I'm aware it may be overwhelming wondering where on earth to start! However, feel free to substitute these questions for anything you have read that especially piques your interest.

1. In your journal, write what you think the perfect space for healing looks like, being mindful of the space you actually have to perform healing in. Would you like some incense burning, or would that be too overpowering? Would you like candlelight, or would you be too distracted by the possibility of a fire breaking out? Do you think it would be more comfortable to be sitting or standing?
2. Perform the "body scanning" techniques from the "preparing for healing" section. How did it feel? Did you notice any areas within your body where your energy felt different? How did you recognise those areas, and why do you think they felt different?
3. Choose at least three of the energy healing methods outlined in the book and spend a week working with each. Make sure you record your experiences. What were the steps you took? How

easy or difficult did you find them? Did you experience any specific sensations or similar whilst working with them? How do you feel at the end of the week compared to the beginning of the week?

4. Imagine you have been asked to perform healing on another person. What steps would you take to perform this? Which method of healing would you use? Would you do anything differently when healing another compared to healing yourself?
5. Are there any of the healing methods that don't appeal to you from what you have learned here? If so, which are they and why do they not appeal to you?
6. Think about the other tools listed. Are there any there that you think you could incorporate into your own healing practices, and if so, how?

CHAPTER FIVE

Building a Cohesive Practice

We have already gone through a lot of information in this book. Whilst knowledge and theory are great, the more you practise and experience, the more you will reap the benefits that energy work has to offer. For the majority of these exercises, I have mentioned the need to practise and perform them "regularly." But with so much to cover and so much to try, where do you start? How can you take what you've learned and use it to build a cohesive practice, one that will benefit you on a day-to-day basis?

I have been a part of several groups in my lifetime and taught both energy work and more pagan practices to a variety of people, often complete beginners. The biggest challenge they all seem to face is finding the time to dedicate to practise. I'm sure we have all been there, and the response most often given is that it should be a "lifestyle change." But what does that mean, and how do we facilitate this lifestyle change to be able to allow us to practise energy work?

These exercises are not something you should consider "separate" from your day-to-day living, but rather ones that are a part of it. The best way to do this is to try and incorporate them into your already established routine and build small but sustainable habits. For example, I often go to the gym in the morning before work and will use the walk to connect with my power centre and focus on strengthening my protective shield. I'll smoke cleanse the house as a part of my weekly cleaning and listen to a crystal sound bath as I shower to aid in cleansing myself. Yes, there are some exercises you will need to put specific time aside for, such as meditation or Qi Gong if you choose to work with those. But even if you can find just five minutes a day and practise them regularly, it will make a difference.

Focus on making small changes that complement your routine whilst you are starting out. The last thing you want to do is become too overzealous, wear yourself out, and then not be able to find the motivation to pick it up again.

Sometimes it can be difficult to maintain a routine, and some people have lives that make it difficult to form a set routine. Maybe you work shifts that change week to week, or maybe you travel regularly for work which means you could be in a different city every month? Even if you feel like your life as a whole lacks routine, we all have our small rituals that we can incorporate energy work into. Perhaps you always have a cup of tea in the morning, whether that's at home or when you get to whichever location you will be at? Making your tea or waiting in line for it could be the perfect opportunity to quickly reflect on something you are grateful for or focus on charging your energy shield.

Elements of a Practice

I recommend focusing on six main elements when building your own cohesive practice: cleansing, protection, connecting, monitoring, healing, and strengthening. Let's break each of these down and see what is involved, and how you can work them into your daily, weekly, or monthly routine to build a sustainable practice.

I have listed these in a linear order, and whilst I recommend that you focus on each element before moving on to the next, there will be exceptions to the rule. For example, if you find yourself in a situation where you are surrounded by negative energy and need protection, then focus on that protection immediately. Don't wait until you can perform a cleanse before you work on your protection. You can always revisit the cleansing step later. Similarly, if you are performing a cleanse and discover a noticeable block in a specific chakra (for example), you can skip straight to the healing rather than needing to perform a protection or a monitoring exercise first. In fact, in these instances it would be wise to perform the healing, then circle back to protection.

So, whilst in an ideal world the order that I have listed is one you should be able to follow step by step, there may be occasions where you need to be flexible. Always listen to your intuition and focus on your immediate needs.

Cleansing

It is important to cleanse regularly. The more negative energy you come into contact with, the more often you will need to cleanse. So how often you want to cleanse depends entirely on how you feel and the amount of negativity you find yourself exposed to. Somebody who works in a high-stress, toxic environment is more likely to need to cleanse more often than someone who tends a garden all day.

The more you practise, the easier it will become to connect with and read your own energy. This will help you understand the signs to look out for that indicate you have negative energy built up and should perform a cleanse. As someone who is quite sensitive to energy, I tend to cleanse once every two or three days.

When you first begin energy work, you may find that you have a lot of negative energy built up that you have never had the tools to banish before. It would make sense for me to tell you that you need to perform a cleanse every day as a beginner to help rid yourself of this negativity. However, we are talking about building a *sustainable* practice. Cleansing every day is not going to be sustainable for many people, even if it is just for a week or two. Little and often is always my recommended approach.

You could turn one of your weekly baths or showers into a cleansing ritual by using a soap infused with herbs associated with cleansing. You could spend a few minutes performing the white light visualisation in the mornings or before bed, or perform a short smoke cleanse. You could even try and incorporate a cleansing exercise whilst you are on the move by listening to a sound bath recording and visualising all of the negative energy leaving your body as you walk or sit on a train to work.

I also tend to cleanse my home anywhere between once a week and once a month, again depending on how the energy of the space feels. These days it is closer to once a month; I very rarely have visitors, and my life is generally peaceful enough (at the moment at least) that I don't feel as though I come home carrying negative energy into the place! I will discuss cleansing the home in more detail in the next chapter.

Protection

Another very important aspect of energy work is protection. The good news is that the more you practise, the stronger your protection will become, and the longer you can go without needing to recharge it. You can use more than one protection method at a time or combine them, depending on what you need.

For example, during those weeks where I have to be in the office most days, I will build and maintain an energy shield. I will usually spend a couple of minutes a day just feeding energy into it, usually whilst I'm walking to the train station or on the train. If at any point during the day I feel it needs some extra power, I will sit at my desk and quietly focus on pulling more energy into my shield to strengthen it. Unfortunately, I am one of those people who work in a fairly intense environment, and so it is not uncommon for me to be surrounded by stressed or unhappy people.

There may be times where you feel you want a bit of added protection in addition to your regular practices. Unfortunately, there are times where we can't avoid having to be involved in toxic situations or avoid being around negative people. In these instances, you could draw a protective symbol on yourself or carry an appropriate crystal or crystal sachet on you to bolster your protection. These can very easily be done in the morning before you head out.

Jewellery can also be used to bring regular protection, and wearing a necklace, a bracelet, or an anklet with a symbol or protection on it—such as a cross or the Hamsa—can be effective. I have a small mirror on a chain I wear when I need some extra protection. I recommend every now and again meditating with your chosen item of jewellery and focusing on imbuing it with the intention of protection to aid in its working.

In terms of protecting the home, I tend to sprinkle salt water around the home, paying attention to the doors and windowsills after I have cleansed my home (which as I said above, can be anywhere between once a week and once a month). I also have my hag stone, which sits by my front door, that I usually meditate with as you would the jewellery every couple of months for added protection. I also like to focus on building a web of protective energy around my home—essentially an energy shield, but one that encompasses my property rather than myself. Again, there is more about protection for the home in the next chapter of the book.

Monitoring

Monitoring is the act of checking your own personal energy. This is to make sure it is staying strong and healthy, and there isn't anything you have missed in your cleanses, or anything that has made its way through your protective methods. Think of it as going to the dentist; at least here in the United Kingdom we tend to go every six months or once a year for a checkup. Any problems spotted are then dealt with by follow-up appointments. In this instance, our monitoring is our checkup, and we can then tailor our healing based on what we find here. However, I do recommend doing this more often than we tend to visit the dentist (and it is much more fun that a trip to the dentist)!

My go-to method is the body scanning technique, as it is quick yet effective. I will usually perform this before bed, roughly once every week or every two weeks. However, you could also use Qi Gong to get in touch with your energy and see if you can sense any blockages. If you work with auras, you could view your aura to gain an idea as to where there may be negativity lurking.

You may even wish to incorporate divination or a pendulum into your monitoring practices, as outlined in the "Other Useful Tools for Energy Healing" section in chapter 4. Asking your pendulum if there are any blockages in your energy and then using the pendulum to narrow down where these are can be a useful monitoring method if you are struggling to connect with your own energy. The more in tune you become with your energetic self, the more likely you are to just "feel" blockages as and when they arise. I personally feel a tightness in my chakras and my energy feels slow and sluggish in that area if any of them are blocked.

When it comes to monitoring, it is especially important to be able to recognize how you personally connect with energy and the symptoms you experience when your energy is off. That way, you can identify these times and then use healing to remedy them.

Healing

When we find those blockages, it is necessary to perform a healing to send healing energy to break down those blockages and strengthen our energetic selves. Exactly how you do this depends on the healing method you prefer to use. You may wish to use a direct approach, such as reiki or EFT tapping, and set aside time specifically to perform this healing.

However, if you are struggling to find the time to dedicate to healing, you may wish to try a more passive approach. For example, you could find a crystal associated with the healing you need and carry it with you or sleep with it under your pillow. You could find a soap or shower gel that includes herbs or scents that correspond with the healing you need and use that as you shower whilst listening to a sound bath recording. I personally find that healing works best when you are free to open yourself up to the healing energies created or channelled; so I do recommend that, where possible, you set time aside specifically for healing.

One thing to mention is that you are more than welcome (and I encourage you) to mix and match healing practices. For example, you could create a crystal grid but incorporate twigs from a specific tree and draw on both crystal and tree energy for your healing. You could choose a crystal that aligns with the healing you need, call on an angel and ask it to fill that crystal with the specific healing that you need, and then carry that crystal around with you. Another option you might want to try is tracing one of the geometric symbols we covered in the crystal grid section over one of your chakras to help unblock and energise it. Never be afraid to experiment and try something new, just because someone hasn't already written about it.

Strengthening

Strengthening is slightly different from healing. With healing, we are focusing on specific areas to remove blockages. Strengthening is instead the act of empowering our energy, keeping it strong and healthy. When we are dehydrated, we may experience a headache, so we will drink water to help hydrate ourselves (healing). However, once we are hydrated again, we will make an effort to keep drinking water to make sure we don't become dehydrated again. This is what I mean by strengthening—it is essentially taking preventative measures to ensure we stay fit and healthy. But in this context, we are talking about fit and healthy in our energetic self.

Strengthening is not that different from healing. You can use these methods to be proactive in keeping your energy healthy, rather than only focusing on using these techniques when a problem does arise. Don't feel that you need to wait until things get bad before you practise the techniques outlined in this book. Strengthening your energy will hopefully mean that it is very rare that it gets to the point where you need to actively focus on healing.

These are all just examples of how you can use the methods in this book to start building your own practice. As you will notice, there are a lot of methods and ways of using energy that I have spoken about in this book that I don't personally use as part of my "standard" routine. However, that doesn't mean that there isn't a time and a place for them, or that I never use them. The more you practise, the more you will understand what works for you, the best methods to help you depending on the specific situation you are facing, and which methods become your regular, go-to methods. It may sound like a lot, but even just a few minutes dedicated to each exercise on a regular basis will really help strengthen your abilities. You may be surprised at how quickly your abilities build up!

Chapter Five Reflections

Building a cohesive practice is not something that will happen overnight; it takes time and dedication. Often, we may think we have come up with the perfect routine, only to put it into practice and realise that it is difficult to integrate it into our everyday lives. We might get frustrated because we aren't seeing results immediately and give up. If you're like me, you might get too excited about building these new habits, try and make too many big changes at once, and end up finding it impossible to keep up with them. This chapter should help you in being able to focus on building and integrating this cohesive practice into your everyday life.

1. Make a list of those activities you perform regularly, whether this is daily or weekly; for example, taking a shower, eating dinner, or commuting to work. Include in this any regular free time you have, such as the period between getting home from work and waiting for your kids to come back from their after-school activities.
2. Think about the elements listed in this chapter: cleansing, protection, monitoring, healing, and strengthening. Look at the list of activities that you perform regularly, and the free time that you have, and see if you can choose one method or technique for each of those elements into those activities/free time.
3. Spend at least a month following your schedule. Make sure that you continue to record your experiences in your journal, and at the end of each week write a summary of how you feel. Then at the end of that month, reflect on how you feel overall. Do you feel any different at the end of the month compared to the beginning of the month? How easy or difficult was it to follow the schedule? Was there anything you would change?
4. Think about situations or activities that may be outside the scope of your usual routine; for example, going on holiday or having to look after your nieces and nephews for a week. How do you anticipate you could maintain a regular practice in those periods where your routine is different?

CHAPTER SIX
Energy and Your Environment

By now, you should have a good grasp as to what energy is and how it works, as well as an understanding of how negative energy can affect us. Energy is all around us, fluid and ever-changing. As such, our environment can have a huge impact on our energetic self. It is extremely important to ensure that we are also paying attention to the energy of our environment. If negative energies are allowed to enter and build up here, they will eventually permeate our internal energetic self and bog us down. Therefore, I wanted to dedicate a portion of this book to managing the energy in your environment, as it would be dangerous to underestimate its importance.

I will mostly be focusing on the home, as this is where the majority of us spend our time. A home can be different for many people. If we live with people we don't get on with (and I have experience of that), it can be a source of stress and maybe even fear. In these situations, especially in house shares, we may only have our bedrooms that we call our safe space. Or we may live in studio flats (again, I have experience of that) where your kitchen or bedroom is crammed into one small space. I have also had experience of living in properties that were dirty, poorly maintained, and physically dangerous (one place had mushrooms growing in the bathroom and half of my bedroom ceiling caved in, but that is a story for another time). I understand that not everyone has the dream "two up/two down," and so we have to work with the space that we've got. If you are sharing your home with others, it is even more important to manage the energy in the space you do have to yourself to ensure you have a safe and harmonious environment to relax and recharge in.

When I moved into my latest flat, I decided to look into feng shui and use that to help harmonise the energies in my home. I instantly fell in love with it, and it has made a huge difference to my spiritual well-being. So I will provide you with a brief introduction to feng shui and some practical ideas as to how you can use it to help balance and optimise the energy of your home. Then we will look at more general cleansing and protection for the home, some of which you may recognise from chapter 3, but more of which will be specific to space rather than our personal selves.

It isn't just the home that we spend a lot of our time in; even with remote working becoming a more readily available option, many of us still spend a lot of time in the office. I personally have never really had my own "office space" and have always worked for companies where hot desking is the norm—so you never have the same desk twice. When considering the office environment, my recommendation would be to focus on your own personal self rather than the environment due to the impermanent nature of this space, so I won't be going into any detail about managing the energy in an office space or more populated spaces.

Feng Shui

Feng shui is an ancient Chinese art of arranging your environment to optimise and harmonise the energies around you. The term *feng shui* roughly translates as "water-wind," which is quite apt considering water is a good conductor of Qi energy and an element that can aid in the flow of this energy.

I remember feng shui becoming popular in the Western world at one point, but this was mostly focused around arranging the home. Traditional feng shui, however, has been used to determine the placement of buildings and structures to create harmony with the local environment, and has a much wider scope than just the home. However, for the purposes of this book, I will be primarily discussing how you can use feng shui in the home. This is because I am sure there are very few readers who are involved in the building of property and structure. Even when it comes to purchasing or renting a home, its particular shape and the directions each room faces is usually of minor consideration compared to its location to transportation and shops and whether it is in a safe area, affordable, and so on.

First, we will discuss the foundations of feng shui that includes using a Bagua map, and how to apply it to your own space. Then I will break down each room and element of the home and what you can do to improve the energies of each space.

I live in a one-bedroom flat, and so I appreciate that space can be restrictive, and often we don't have a choice as to where we put a desk or a chair. However, I have found that incorporating even the most basic of feng shui elements can have a huge impact on the energy of the home, and this in turn will have a positive effect on your own energetic self.

One thing to note before we move forward is that symmetry is greatly admired, but again I appreciate that due to space constraints, it can be difficult to achieve this. But do bear this in mind when placing plants, ornaments, or furniture.

The Bagua Map

I will be focusing specifically on the Three Gate Bagua map, as this is the one most commonly used and is in my opinion easier to interpret. It is essentially a grid split into different areas of life (such as family and creativity), and this can be used to demonstrate how the different areas of your home represent the different areas of your life. This can help you determine the optimal layout of your home to allow you to really enhance and embrace its energetic potential.

There are two types of Bagua map. In the first, the grid is drawn as an octagon, an eight-sided shape, split into eight sections (triangles):

The top section of the octagon represents fame and recognition (associated with the south, despite it traditionally being shown at the top of the map).

The second section (moving clockwise around the Bagua from the top section) represents relationships, love, marriage, and friendship (southwest).

The third section represents children and creativity (west).

The fourth section represents travel, neighbours, and "helpful people" (northwest).

The fifth section (at the bottom of the octagon) represents the career (north).

The sixth section represents knowledge, learning, and wisdom (northeast).

The seventh section represents health and the family (east).

The eighth section represents money and wealth (southeast).

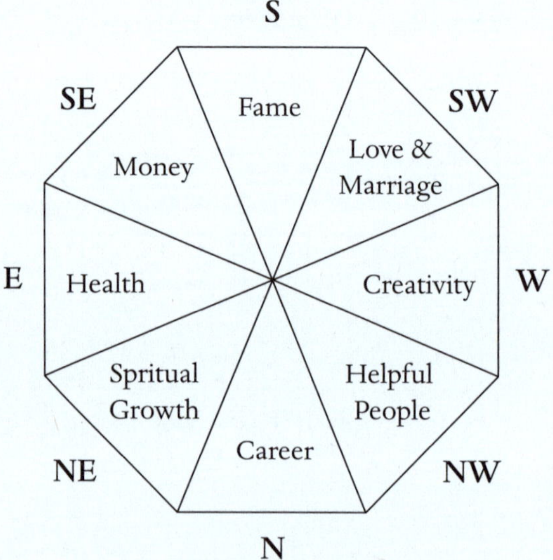

Figure 29: Three Gate Bagua Map

You may also see the map drawn as a large square, with three rows of three squares inside, so nine sections in all. The octagon is used in traditional Eastern feng shui, whilst the square pattern has been adopted by Western feng shui. It is up to you which you decide to work with based on your knowledge, experience, and comfort level. From left to right, these squares represent:

Top row—Left hand square: Wealth and money. Middle Square: Fame and recognition. Right hand square: Relationships, love, marriage, and friendship

Middle row—Left hand square: Family. Middle square: Health and well-being. Right hand square: Creativity

Bottom row—Left hand square: Knowledge, learning, and wisdom. Middle square: Career. Right hand square: Helpful people and travel

Wealth & Prosperity	Fame & Reputation	Love & Marriage
Family & Ancestors	Health & Center	Children & Creativity
Knowledge & Self-cultivation	Career & Life Path	Helpful People & Travel

Figure 30: Bagua Map

To use the Bagua map, you will need an accurate, to-scale floor plan of your home. You will also need to scale the Bagua map so that it fits inside your floor plan. Place this over the Bagua map, with the wall that contains the door you enter your house or flat along the bottom (so your door will fall either in the career, knowledge, or helpful people section). From here, you should be able to see which areas of your house best support the different areas of the Bagua map. For example, the room that aligns with family could be perfect to make into a living room. If you desire more money and the room that aligns with that area is your kitchen, hang wealth charms or keep a money bowl in the kitchen.

Again, I appreciate that this isn't always possible, and some of us have to make do with the space we have. Sometimes these can be contradictory. For example, feng shui states that the bedroom should be a place of romance and peace, and you should avoid anything mentally stimulating in the bedroom (even as far as removing books from the bedroom). However, my bedroom falls in the knowledge area. Living in a small, one-bedroom flat, there is no way I can move the bedroom anywhere else. Similarly, the only suitable space for my working desk is in the "creativity" area, and the only suitable place for my living room (which is where I knit, paint, etc.) is in the career area. It would be mighty uncomfortable to move these spaces around; if I move my desk to the "career" area, the light from the window will cause too much glare, and if I move my sofa to the "creativity" area I'll never be able to open the doors of the Juliet balcony! As such, I have unfortunately had to discount the Bagua map for a different approach.

Feng shui also emphasises that every space should be "separate" if possible, or well defined, as each will have its own energy. For example, your kitchen and bedroom should be separate, your study and living room or study and bedroom should also be separate. Again, this isn't possible for me, and my living room has to double as my study. However, using a TV unit and some plants, I have effectively "divided" the room into two distinct spaces without making them feel closed in or interrupting the flow of Qi around the space. If I had used a floor-to-wall bookcase instead of the TV unit, this would definitely show a separation between the space, but it would essentially create a wall that would block the flow of Qi around the apartment. In this instance, I listened to my intuition and connected with the energy of the space to understand exactly what it needed. When in doubt, listen to your own intuition and what makes your own energy feel flowing and free.

This leads us nicely on to looking at the different spaces your home might have, and how to foster positive energies throughout each.

The Front Door/Hallway

The front door is called the mouth of the Qi, as this is where the Qi enters the home. It is the first thing we see when we enter the house, so it needs to be inviting and clutter free. If energies are blocked here, then it will have a knock-on effect on the energy's ability to travel around the home.

Placing a plant on either side of the door helps improve the energies, as does having a water feature by the front door (preferably with running or flowing water than stagnant water). I have a potted plant on the shoe rack as you walk into the entrance through my front door, as well as an amethyst-infused lavender and vanilla diffuser to create an inviting scent. Anything you can do to minimise the clutter—shoes racks, coat hooks, shelving—will help this area.

For those who live in houses, often you open the front door and the staircase to the upper level will be in front of you. This is not ideal in feng shui, as it funnels the Qi upstairs before it has had a chance to flow through the downstairs. You can slow this energy flow down, giving it ample time to spread, by blocking the view of the stairs from the doorway by placing a plant or similar at its base. If this isn't possible, a rug or a chandelier-type light will catch the Qi and slow it down.

The Living Room

The living room is considered a yin space. Generally, it is a place where the family gathers, and so the seating should be arranged to allow for this. In contrast to how many modern living rooms are set up, the TV should not be the focal point. Try positioning the chairs or sofas facing one another with the TV at the end, rather than having them all focused toward the TV. For someone like me, who just has the one sofa, this isn't really feasible! But if you live in a family home, then this setup is the recommended approach. Sofas and chairs should be made from a comfortable fabric, and they should also not be positioned so you and your guests have your backs facing the door where possible.

Balance is important in living spaces. If you have a large living room, or perhaps a space that serves as both a living room and a kitchen or a living room and a dining room, try to use furniture and other items to make a clear delineation between the different spaces. I've given the example of my living room which also has to double as my study; so I've used a TV cabinet and some plants to clearly divide the space without cutting it off. This way I have a space that is dedicated to learning and mental faculties, and a space dedicated to relaxation and sociability, all within the same room.

If your living room is small, try to keep furniture low to stop the room from appearing top heavy. If you can't do this, make sure any arrangement you have focuses on larger, heavier items being toward the bottom of the furniture. For example, if you have a bookcase that stands from floor to ceiling, have all your larger, heavier books at the bottom, and the smaller books on the upper shelves (or even just ornaments on the upper shelves instead).

If you have a fireplace in your living room (or any room), then this provides Qi with a means of escape, so place a mirror above it.

The Dining Room

The dining room is yet another social area, and it is also considered to be a place of wealth and abundance.

The shape of the table you have in your dining room can be important. A round table tends to force the Qi to spin around the guests, which can feel a bit chaotic. Rectangular tables can alienate those sat at the ends. Square tables are ideal, as are octagonal tables. If you wish to hang a mirror in the dining room, do not hang it so that any seated guests are staring into it as they eat, as this can make them feel self-conscious and distracted. Remember that the dining room is a place you eat, so keep anything that may cause feelings of discomfort around eating practices out of this space; this could include portraits of hunting scenes, maybe even fashion magazines that promote unhealthy body standards, or that banana at the bottom of the fruit bowl you forgot about and is now going mouldy.

The Kitchen

The kitchen is said to be one of the more difficult spaces to manage in feng shui, and I completely relate to this. My kitchen is small; I mean, my whole flat is small, but my kitchen is especially small. I am not exaggerating when I say there is no room to swing a cat! The main reason that a kitchen can be difficult is due to the many functions it can play; it can be a place for preparing and cooking food, for family and friends to come and gather, for children to play if it is a larger space, or for some who have a dining and kitchen arrangement, it can also act as an office. As such, it can be difficult to accommodate all of these energies and know exactly which ones to optimise.

The energy of the kitchen can also depend on your relationships with food and cooking. If you love cooking, then it can be a space where you can relax and be creative. If you hate cooking, it is simply a place of convenience. If you are into nutrition and have a healthy relationship with food, you will probably spend more time in the kitchen creating healthy meals and organising your food spaces. For those who don't have a good relationship with food, the kitchen can be a source of misery and shame, perhaps one that we try and avoid.

Like all spaces, the Qi should feel free to move harmoniously around the space. If you have your kitchen door facing outside doors or windows, this will just funnel the Qi straight through—similar to our front door and our staircase—and so putting something in the way can help slow this energy down. I have always found that plants on the windowsill is a great way to slow down energy, but other ornaments and features will also help.

If, like me, you have a smaller kitchen then the opposite is more likely to happen; the energy feels stagnant with little space to move around. This is especially prevalent in kitchens of a darker colour; whilst my walls are white and the worktop is a light marble colour, the oven is black, the tiling behind it is grey, and all my shelving units and drawers are black. Square corners are also considered harsh and can interrupt the flow of Qi, and the kitchen is one of the areas you will most likely encounter this thanks to worktops, appliances, and cupboards and drawers.

Try to add a brighter colour theme to the kitchen; this could be with lighter coloured appliances, plants, some nice artwork or wall hangings such as sun catchers. Try to cover up sharp corners as much as possible, although I will admit, this is not something I have successfully managed to achieve in my own kitchen!

As we have seen, it is best to try and minimise clutter where possible, which again can be especially difficult in small kitchens. Get smart with your storage; hang your pots and pans or knives from the wall, ensure that you aren't hoarding out-of-date food, and optimise corner spaces with open corner shelving to help to declutter the space.

The Bedroom

The main focus of the bedroom should be relaxation and rejuvenation, and it is also associated with bringing romance into our lives.

Ideally, the bed should be positioned so that you have a view of the doorway, but not directly facing the door. In China, having the foot of the bed in line with the doorway is known as the mortuary position, because this is how coffins are placed when they are awaiting collection. It is also not ideal to have windows facing one another, or windows and doors facing one another. This is especially difficult if this alignment crosses over the bed, as this particular arrangement is said to cause sickness.

Furniture should be raised to allow for energy to flow under and around it. Preferably the frame should be made from natural materials, such as wood.

Mirrors in the bedroom should not be facing the bed, and as always, clutter should be kept to a minimum. If you have anything larger than a single bed, you want to ensure balance by maintaining symmetry; if you have a bedside table at one side of the bed, you will want a matching one on the other side, for example.

Electronics are said to be less than ideal in the bedroom, as they can distract from the main purpose of the space (relaxation). However, I personally am a bit more casual with this rule and have compromised by keeping a small projector in my room that I can plug in and set up when I want to use it. I also use my phone for my alarm and to listen to meditation music to lull me to sleep, so keeping this out of the room is not really an option.

Books should also be kept out of the bedroom, as these are mentally stimulating and not conducive to the relaxing, romantic environment we wish to muster. Instead focus on decorations such as candles, ornaments, and anything with sentimental value (such as a stuffed animal given to you by a parent) that will encourage loving energies.

The Bathroom

In feng shui, the element of water is associated with wealth, and where else do we use the majority of our water but in the bathroom? As such, make sure that you don't have any dripping or leaking taps or clogged drains, as this can represent your wealth being washed away or becoming blocked.

Ideally you don't want the bathroom being the first thing that visitors see when they come in, and you don't want the toilet to be the first thing you see when you enter the bathroom. However, again this is not always possible—my bathroom is directly opposite the front door, and the toilet is the very first thing you see! It is recommended that you keep the bathroom door completely closed, but this makes my space feel very restrictive and oppressive. As such, I have opted to keep the door half closed so the toilet isn't visible, and I have focused on making the entrance to my flat as welcoming as possible, so visitors focus on that first rather than the bathroom. Remember, the ultimate goal of feng shui is to make the space feel as energetically free and positive as possible, so don't blindly follow the "rules" if they result in you feeling uncomfortable in your space.

Unfortunately, my bathroom has no windows and is tiled completely in grey. Even with the light on, it feels very dingy and oppressive. I have hung a large mirror to make the space feel bigger, and have also opted for storage under the sink, utilising the space there rather than adding cabinets or shelving that would stick out and make the space feel smaller. There is very little opportunity to make the space seem brighter or lighter, so instead I've leaned into it and gone for a more "dreamlike" space of relaxation. I have battery-powered candles I use when bathing rather than using the main lights, which feel harsh in such a small space, and I have some sea-scented potpourri and some crystals to decorate the space.

The Office

With working from home or hybrid working becoming more popular now, many of us will need some sort of office space in our homes. Online research is key for many of us; from writing books such as this to using YouTube to find video tutorials to learn a new hobby, many people have a dedicated computer space that could be considered a "study" for all intents and purposes. In this section, I will be talking predominantly about personal home offices; if you use your home office to actually meet with clients and other external visitors, then the guidance will be slightly different. Due to it not being one I have any experience with, I will not be covering it here.

The study is one of the most important spaces to try and keep "separate." Not only do you not want to be faced with distractions whilst you are trying to work, but you also want to be able to walk away from it at the end of the day and psychologically "switch off" from work mode.

You don't want the desk facing the window, as this too can cause a distraction. If you do have the desk facing a window or a door, place something to minimise the distraction; curtains, plants, hanging decorations. Plants are ideal in a study space if you are using computers, as they are associated with yin energies and can help balance out the yang energies of the technology. This is especially relevant if your work is very technology heavy (my full-time job is in technology, so I tend to have my laptop, my computer, keyboard, mouse, microphone, Wi-Fi hub, headphones, and two monitors on the go when I'm working).

In my experience, the desk is one of the easiest places to become cluttered; trailing cables, empty glasses and plates, books, pens, or notebooks can all build up rather quickly! Use cable ties to gather and hide wiring, and a desk organiser to store pens and notebooks in. Try to get into the habit of disposing of any other items as and when you have used them—take your plate back to the kitchen, put that book back on the shelf, as you go to ensure your desk space remains uncluttered.

As well as not letting clutter build up, you also don't want to see physical reminders of your workload building up. Whilst a board with sticky notes listing everything you need to do can help you remain organised, it can also be a visual reminder of how much work you have to do. This can be overwhelming and difficult to switch off from at the end of the day. Try to store any lists, papers, and forms, away at the end of the day so you aren't accidentally noticing them when you are trying to relax.

General

The following list provides some more general guidance used in feng shui to help you ensure that Qi can flow freely around your space. Remember, this is just guidance; do not worry if it is difficult to achieve these within the space you have. Ensuring that you feel that your energy aligns with the energy of your space is the most important element here.

Edges and Corners—As discussed in the other sections, edges can feel harsh, and corners can feel dark and cavernous, which can disrupt the energy flow. Use plants, coverings, ornaments, and other features to fill and distract from these areas.

Scent—Scents can be used to help optimise the energies. I personally have some diffuser sticks on the shoe rack so the minute you enter the flat you experience a lovely lavender and vanilla scent. I also burn sandalwood essential oil in the bedroom when I have had a particularly bad day to help cleanse and calm me.

Mirrors—Again, we have touched on mirrors in several of the previous sections. Mirrors can be used to make a space seem bigger but should not be hung where a guest will have no choice but to stare at themselves in it. You should also not hang mirrors directly opposite a door or a window, as it is believed that the Qi will reflect off the mirror and out through that door or window. Mirrors can also be used in dark or small spaces to encourage movement in stagnant energy, and conversely convex mirrors can be used in larger spaces to slow energy down.

If you are exploring feng shui and looking for ways to express this in your living space, you might come across Bagua mirrors. These should never be hung inside the home, only outside of the home to protect from negative energies entering in.

Materials—Remember, balance is very important in feng shui, and materials can help us achieve that balance. Hard, reflective surfaces such as bathroom tiles or kitchen worktops have a yang energy and allow Qi to move quickly. Softer materials such as fabrics, with a lighter feel and colour are associated with yin energy and move more slowly. It is important to strive for balance between these when decorating your space.

Beds are a great example of where this can easily be achieved; hard, metallic, or wooden frames are associated with yang energy, whereas the soft covers and pillows we place on them represent the yin energy. In my study space, I have my wooden desk and my computer and other technological components (Yang energy), such as a soft, pastel pink mouse pad that takes up most of the desk, and some pottery and goddess figurines to represent yin energy.

Plants—You will see that I recommend plants a lot; this is because they bring good energies into the home and can help purify the air. Even different plants have different energies; plants with soft, drooping leaves are considered to represent yin energy, whereas those with upright, spiky leaves represent yang energy. They can be used to bring colour into a space, hide sharp edges, brighten up dark corners, and slow down Qi energy.

Lighting—Lighting can play a huge part in our mental and physical well-being. Dim lighting when we are trying to focus can strain our eyes and make us feel tired, whereas bright lighting when we are trying to relax can make us feel too switched on. Our bodies naturally tune in with the rising and setting of the sun and recognising and emulating this can really help. Consider the purpose of each room and the most suitable lighting. As we have said, for those areas where you are wanting to relax, such as the bedroom, dim lighting is more appropriate than bright. However, in areas such as the kitchen or the study where you need to focus, the lighting needs to be adequate to allow you to do so.

One thing I cannot live without in the winter is my sunrise lamp. I set it before I go to bed to correspond with my alarm, and wake to a "sunrise" effect, a soft light that slowly glows brighter. This feels a much more welcome start to the day than switching on a bright light!

Encourage natural lighting where you can, and position yourself so you can make the most of this. For example, if you spend most of your time working or studying from home, place your desk in a spot where you will get the most natural light without it being glaring. If you tend to spend most of your time in the living room, arrange your furniture as to not block any of that natural light coming in.

Cleansing Your Space

Our space is also susceptible to picking up and harbouring negative energies. It is important to keep our space cleansed as well as our own selves. Many of the cleansing methods we have already mentioned can be modified to suitably cleanse the home. Below are the ones I personally find are the most effective when used on a space.

Sound Vibration

Sound waves are energy, and the vibration of this energy can be used to cleanse and heal not just yourself but also your space. A small bell or anything that "chimes" works well. Walk around your space in a clockwise direction as you ring the bell, visualising the vibration of the sound chasing out any negative energies.

Smoke Cleanse

You can smoke cleanse your space as well as yourself (I will usually combine these and smoke cleanse myself and then my space whilst I'm at it). This is one of my preferred methods to cleanse a space, due to its simplicity.

Performing a Smoke Cleanse

Take your incense and walk around your space in a clockwise direction whilst wafting the smoke around, making sure you cover all areas, even the corners and other nooks and crannies. You may wish to use the same chant for cleansing your space; I tend to repeat the following as I go:

"I cleanse this space of all negativity, in this world and in the astral.
I cleanse this space of all negativity, in this world and in the astral.
May all negative energies be banished from the place.
May only love and light be permitted to enter this space.
I cleanse this space of all negativity, in this world and in the astral."

I usually only walk around the place once, unless it has been a while since I last cleansed. In that case, I will walk the space three times, repeating the above as I go, almost like a "deep clean."

Cleansing Spray

You can create your own cleansing spray. Making your own spray is easy enough. All you need is water, essential oils associated with cleansing (such as peppermint, lemon, rosemary, or lavender), vodka, and a container to store it in.

Add the water to the container, followed by a small amount of vodka to stop the oil from separating from the water. Then add a few drops of your chosen essential oils, give it a good shake, and you're ready to start using it. I recommend just using essential oils and avoiding adding herbs to the mixture; I have found that herbs tend to discolour the water, and the last thing you want to do is stain the walls of your home!

Salt Water

Salt water is a great cleanser. Simply mix three pinches of salt with water and sprinkle it in a clockwise direction around your space, paying particular attention to entries/exits, such as doors and windows. This mixture also doubles as protection against negative energies as well as cleansing any which may already be present, so is especially potent for such a simple method.

Floor Washes

If your space has a hardwood floor, then you can create a wash to mop the floor with to cleanse the space. Add rosemary and a few drops of lemon juice (or add some peel of a lemon) to your water—or you can use essential oils—and mop the floor starting from the centre of the room and working out toward the door. As you do, see yourself washing away any negative energies. Similarly, if you don't want to mop, you can use a broom and visualise yourself sweeping those negative energies away.

Protecting Your Space

As with cleansing, there are several of the protection methods we mentioned above that you can use to help protect your space, as well as some additional ones. The ones that I most commonly recommend are included in this section.

Crystals

You can create a crystal grid for protection and keep it near the entrance of your house, or in a specific room if there is a specific area you wish to protect. Take a look at the crystal grid layouts covered in the crystal healing section of chapter 4 for more information on building a crystal grid. Crosses and Metatron's grid are good ones to try if you wish to experiment with grids for protection.

Charms and Talismans

Charms and talismans are great to hang around your space to bring protection. Hag stones—stones with a natural hole through—are associated with protection. I have one that I keep on the shoe rack near my front door to bring protection to my home. Other popular items you could use include the Hamsa and witch's bells.

Salt

Salt is great for protecting a space. Simply sprinkle it across your doorways and windowsills to prevent any negative energies from entering. You may wish to use black salt instead of regular salt for this exercise. Black salt is salt that has been mixed with charcoal to give it that extra protective "oomph." This can easily be made by yourself by grinding sea salt, incense ash, and charcoal together.

Ley Lines

We have discussed energy in our internal environment, but the energy of our external environment also needs to be considered and understood. Ley lines are essentially energetic power lines that flow beneath the earth. There are hundreds of them across the world connecting some of the most iconic ancient structures and monuments.

Ley lines were a concept "discovered" by Alfred Watkins.[14] Watkins proposed in the 1920s that these ley lines were actually "sighting lines" rather than the energy highways they are known as today (that would come later in the 1960s). It is well known that the shortest distance between two places is a straight line, and pre-Roman times there would have been a need for an easy way to navigate between key locations across the country, for trade and such. These ley lines were just that, and the route of the ley was marked by a range of features to help guide travellers along them.

According to Watkins, the earliest lines were most likely from natural mountain peak to natural mountain peak of at least 1,000 feet. With such

14. Alfred Watkins, *The Old Straight Track: Its Mounds, Beacons, Moats, Sites and Mark Stones* (Heritage Hunter, 2016), Kindle.

a distance, these would be impossible to navigate by foot, so secondary sighting points were made that could be easily noticed by a person standing at the previous sighting point, all in a straight line.

These secondary sighting points were marked by a number of different monuments. These included the below:

Cairns and Stones—Large standing stones, or cairns made up of a tower of stones, were often used as markers. They were often erected at burial mounds or as memorials as well as general markers.

Castles—Similar to churches, Watkins also noted that many castles were built across ley lines and so considered these as markers also.

Churches—Many ancient churches were built over places that were previously considered sacred, and Watkins noted that their placement often correlated with the ley lines he discovered.

Mounds—A mound is a heap of earth, rock, or other debris. Often these were artificial, for example burial mounds built by our ancestors. Their height would have made them ideal markers or sighting points.

Moats—A moat is a deep, wide ditch often built as a defence around a building or a town. Often in dry seasons moats would dry up, revealing roads beneath them, meaning that they could be used for travel as well as acting as an obvious marker. This same logic applies to ponds also.

Trees—There are many trees that have stood since ancient times. There is the Ankerwycke Yew in Berkshire, which is believed to be up to 2,500 years old; the Major Oak in Nottinghamshire, which is believed to be up to 1,000 years old for example. These would have been known to our ancestors and used as a marker, or a sighting point, along a ley line.

Wells—Water wells, which were more prevalent in ancient times than they are today, were also considered by Watkins to have been used as sighting points.

Many of these monuments don't exist today. In his work *The Old Straight Track: Its Mounds, Beacons, Moats, Sites and Mark Stones,* place names can be a good indicator as to where these could have existed.[15] For example, the suffix *-ton,* such as in "Southampton," could indicate a stone marker was once present there, which a building or even town was then built around. Old sarsen stones have been found in Southampton, which are blocks of quartzite, and this type of stone was used to build Stonehenge (as well as dolerite). This includes a large sarsen stone weighing half a ton that was present at the side of the road near what is now Southampton Common—perhaps this could have been a prominent marker in ancient times?

Watkins also suggested that the suffix *-bury* could indicate a mound, perhaps a burial mound, and the suffix *-low* held similar meaning in Derbyshire. The suffix *-tree* could indicate an ancient tree that was used as a sighting in this area.

Watkins made this discovery by accident. Following a visit to Blackwardine, he saw whilst looking at a map a straight line starting from Croft Ambury, through Blackwardine, over Risbury, and through Stretton Grandison that ended at a Roman station. To him, this straight line and the hilltops and such it ran through led to this intriguing theory. So, he grabbed a map and circled all of the natural points, such as hills and mounds, as well as ancient churches, castles, moats, ponds, ancient stones, wells, and other notable landmarks. By sticking a pin in one of these, placing a straight edge (such as ruler) against it, and then moving it around until four or more of these places lined up, he found a large number of these lines—more than he believed could be called coincidental.

In fact, you can search for ley lines yourself using this method. Even today new ley lines are being discovered using this approach. Just grab yourself a map, a pen, and do a bit of research into ancient monuments in

15. Watkins, *The Old Straight Track.*

the area you are looking at. See what you can come up with. You may not find anything new, but it is still fun to map them out yourself and see them all align.

Watkins's introduction of ley lines assigned them a very practical purpose. In the 1960s, these took on a more spiritual and energetic meaning, largely thanks to the works of John Michell.[16]

The most well-known ley line in the United Kingdom is the Saint Michael's ley line. Now, there are actually two Saint Michael ley lines that intersect at an axis at St. Michael's Mount in Cornwell.

The first we will discuss is the Saint Michael's ley line also known as the Apollo Line. This line was publicised by Jean Richer in the late 1950s. This line connects monasteries that have been dedicated to St. Michael right across Europe and the Middle East. This line stretches from Ireland, through Cornwell, France, Italy, Greece, Cyprus, through to Israel. It is also said that this ley line perfectly aligns with the sunset of the summer solstice (Northern Hemisphere), although this has been shown to be incorrect.

The second of these lines runs exclusively through Britain, from St. Michael's Mount in Cornwall, through Brentnor, Burrowbridge Mump, Glastonbury Tor, the Avebury Henge, and Bury St. Edmunds, through to Hopton on the coast.

There are many other ley lines in the United Kingdom and indeed across the world. There is one in Herefordshire that stretches from Longtown Castle, through Arthur's Stone, Weobley Castle, Pembridge Church, and Wigmore Church and Castle. There is also one in York that passes through St. Samson's Church, St. Mary Castlegate, and the site of a now-demolished Templar Chapel.

I used to live in Winchester, which has a ley line that runs from Tidbury Ring near Bullington Cross, through the remains of a barrow close to South Wonston, before heading into Winchester and passing through the Cathedral, on to St. Catherine's Hill, and ending in Twyford. I loved

16. John Michell, *The View Over Atlantis* (Abacus, 1973).

climbing to the top of St. Catherine's Hill and just soaking up the energy—it was clearly a place of power. Once you become more attuned to the energy within you and the energy around you, you will soon be able to notice when you are standing on a ley line!

Of course, ley lines are controversial. The number of these sorts of monuments as defined by Watkins is huge in the United Kingdom, and the principle of finding ley lines can be assigned to anything. A man called Matthew Parker mapped out a dozen Woolworths stores across the United Kingdom, showing them connecting in a perfectly symmetrical straight line. Whilst I get the sentiment (and I did have a good chuckle over the Woolworth's alignment), I have found my own experiences of ley lines to be a powerful one, encapsulating an energy unlike you often experience.

There are many books that list known ley lines throughout the world, as well as online resources. You can have a go at finding your own using the pin in the map method that Watkins himself used. You can also dowse for ley lines using a pendulum or dowsing rods; when stood over a ley line, your tool should display a change in behaviour, such as dowsing rods pointing downward or your pendulum swinging more so than it usually does.

I'll be honest, I have never been able to get on with dowsing. I have tried it on and off for years, using different pendulums made of different materials, but it is just one of those practices I have never been able to master, so whether this is accurate or not is not for me to say. However, I always very strongly feel the energy of these sacred places. They are great to go and recharge your own energy, and to tap into the collective energy that flows around us. Practising your cleansing and general energy work in such places can have a really profound effect, so I urge you to see if there are any ley lines near you and give it a try.

Ley lines are fantastic sources of energy, but they are not the only natural sources of energy. As we have discussed, energy can linger in a place, even temporarily. We can use these places to aid us in our energy work too. I'm sure many of us are familiar with the concepts of altars and shrines; a place, or structure (such as a table) that is considered holy. One of the reasons that people build such structures is to create a space where spiritual workings can take place. Often simply sitting at your altar or shrine can bring a sense of peace and spiritual connection. This is in part due to the energy that has built up there through its use, having been imprinted with that particular intention.

This "imprinting" of intention can also happen accidentally when a particular space is used regularly in a specific way. In this sense, many places can become "ley lines" of sorts. Maybe there is a specific walk you and a partner or you and your family take every Sunday after dinner? If so, focus on the feelings of love and joy you feel by spending this time with your loved ones as you walk, and let it meld with the energy of the place. Over time, you will find that this particular location that you take your walks becomes almost like a personal ley line, and one which you can walk when you need to tap into those feelings; maybe you have had a bad day, or maybe your family has gone away to visit relatives and you wish to connect with their energy whilst they are gone.

In a city I used to live in several years ago, there was a large park toward the centre. There was one particular path, off the beaten track, that each year would be full of magpies during the summer; clearly it was a popular place for magpies to build their nests. At a certain point in the year, you could walk down it and find yourself surrounded by a great number of magpies, more than I could count, flying between the tree branches or foraging for food along the path. I have always felt there is something quite special about magpies—I even have a magpie tattoo on my arm, as I feel such an affinity with this creature. As such, walking this path and watching the magpies always felt like a spiritual experience, and I loved the energy of the place when it was full. So even if you don't live near any ley lines, there is nothing stopping you from creating or discovering your own, localised, places of power or spaces where you can connect more strongly with energies if you wish.

Creating Your Own Healing Sanctuary

If you don't want to wait to find that external space with the energies necessary to draw upon for healing, then you can create your own. To do this, we will need to find our space and then focus on imbuing it with the energies of healing. It is important that you focus on this before you begin to take healing energies from it. If you don't, you will be drawing on the energy of the place, yes, but it won't be as powerful in your healing without the intention of healing already programmed into it.

First, choose your location. Whilst it is tempting to choose somewhere far from prying eyes, please consider your personal safety first and foremost. I recommend choosing somewhere already rooted in nature, easy to access, but not too secluded. A specific tree you can sit under in your local park would work well.

There are many ways you can help to bring healing energies to the spot you have chosen. I will list several that appear from this book. I would like you to choose at least three and perform them at your chosen space. I recommended that you perform one, then wait at least three days before returning to your chosen spot and performing the next. If you can think of any other methods or have any ideas that I have not listed here, then please use that as one of your three.

1. Perform the roots meditation. Focus on taking healing energy down from the sky, through your body, out through your feet, and into the earth. Concentrate on this energy being stored in the earth for when you need it.
2. Perform the energy orb exercise. Focus on filling your orb with healing energy. When you feel ready, place the orb into the ground so that healing energy can be absorbed by the earth.
3. Take a small number of healing crystals with you and create a crystal grid in the space. Make sure you take the crystals with

you when you leave, as these could present a danger to wildlife if left.

4. Invoke reiki energy, draw the Cho Kei Rei symbol into the ground, and send this reiki energy into the earth via your hands. Focus on this energy being stored in the earth.
5. Invoke a specific angel and send angelic healing energy into the earth via your hands. Again, focus on this energy being stored in the earth.
6. Choose a planetary energy and create a symbol of healing using this planet's magic square. Etch this symbol into the ground and focus on the healing energy of this planet soaking into, and being stored in, the earth.
7. Create "healing water" from the "healing with natural spirits" section and pour this into the ground.

Before you perform any of these exercises, head to your chosen space and just spend a bit of time in meditation, connecting with the energy. Make a note in your journal as to how it feels. After you have performed each of your three exercises, take a moment to again connect with the energy of the space and see if it has changed at all. Once you have completed all three exercises, connect with it again, and record any changes you experience in your journal.

I recommend that you perform at least one exercise every month in your chosen space, especially if you are using it to conduct energy healing regularly. Over time, you should find that this becomes an energetically sacred space, one that can bring peace and rejuvenation just by being in its presence. Make sure that you always treat this area with respect (do not litter or leave anything behind for example), and enjoy this healing space you have created.

Chapter Six Reflections

Whilst this book primarily focuses on healing the energy of an individual through the various methods we have discussed, it is extremely important to manage the energies of your external environment. Whilst the effect that external energies can have on our own, internal energy is often acknowledged, I personally feel it isn't discussed in enough depth. Through this chapter you should have learned more about these energies and how we can manage them to ensure peace and harmony within our energetic self.

1. Take at least one of the rooms in your house. Using the principles of feng shui, how could you rearrange it to best create harmony in that space?
2. Cleanse at least one space in your house (if not the whole house). How did you do it, and does your space feel any different than before you performed it?
3. Protect at least one room or space in your house (if not the whole house). How did you do it, and does your space feel any different than before you performed it?
4. Do a bit of research and make a list of any ley lines or sacred places in your local area. Visit one and record your experience. Could you feel any difference in the energy between that place and other places? Were there any sensations you experienced? How do you think you could tap into and use this energy?
5. Whether you are near any ley lines or not, are there any places near you that you could consider to be a "personal" place of power? If not, can you think of any way you could go about creating one of these, and consider how you might use it in your future practice?

Closing Words

As you may have gathered from this book, there have been many cultures and civilisations over hundreds of years that have recognised not only that this universal energy exists, but the importance of it to both ourselves and the world around us. Whilst there has been a lot we have covered in this book, even now we are only just scratching the surface of working with energy and the different ways we can use this energy to heal ourselves and others. The world in general is becoming more aware of this energy. More and more people are waking up to the possibilities that are open to us when we embrace this energy and use it to work for the highest good.

Whilst the information in this book covers some of the most well-known energy and energy healing practices, as with all things, trust your intuition. Don't be afraid to wander from the beaten track. I have had experiences and use certain symbols and such to aid me in healing that I haven't listed here. This is because they have been gifted to me through meditation, journeying, and practice that are very personal to me, and I cannot say with certainty would work for anyone else. Despite the wealth of information that exists on healing, cleansing, and protection, there will always be more to discover and more to learn.

This path is one of wonder, promise, and empowerment. However, it won't always be easy, for if it was then everyone would be doing it! There will be days where you doubt yourself; maybe you don't feel like a healing has worked, maybe you've been too busy to keep up with your practices, or maybe you find yourself wondering if any of this is even real? Doubt is good; it is a sign of progress and growth. Blindly following without stopping to question what you are doing or where you are going very rarely does us any good.

Remember, these are teachings that could stick with you for the rest of your life, so never feel guilty or unworthy if you don't feel as though you are giving it 100 percent all of the time. Sometimes the best thing we can do for our energetic selves is just to stop, sit back, and take a break. Never compare your experiences to someone else's and wonder what you are doing wrong. As I keep emphasising, everybody experiences these things differently. I experience chakras as colour, my friend experiences them as vibration only. I cannot connect with the energy of the hematite crystal to save my life, but another friend loves the protective energy it provides. Nobody else can walk your path but you, so do so with confidence and curiosity and strength in your sense of self.

My intention with this book was to open the door to energy work; to give you a taste of the various methods and tools we can incorporate into our practices so that you may experience this connection and its benefits for yourself. That you may search wider than this book at all that is out there and build a practice that is truly your own, one which you benefit from on a daily basis. This energy is all around us, and being able to recognize it and work with it is a wonderful gift that can truly enrich our lives. I hope after reading you feel the same, and I wish you all the best in your journey along this path!

Recommended Reading

Campion, Lisa. *The Art of Psychic Reiki: Developing Your Intuitive and Empathetic Abilities for Energy Healing.* New Harbinger, 2019.

Forest, Danu. *Celtic Tree Magic: Ogham Lore and Druid Mysteries*. Llewellyn Publications, 2014.

Hall, Judy. *Encyclopaedia of Crystals*. Fair Winds Press, 2013.

Howard, Jessica. *Meditations to Soothe the Soul*. Published by the author, 2024.

Jones, Katina Z. *The Little Book of Feng Shui: A Room-by-Room Guide to Energize, Organize, and Harmonize Your Space.* Adams Media, 2020.

Judith, Anodea. *Wheels of Life: A User's Guide to the Chakra System.* Llewellyn Publishing, 2012.

Lizos, George. *Protect Your Light: A Practical Guide to Energy Protection, Cleansing, and Cutting Cords*. Red Wheel/Weiser, 2022.

Shaw, Scott. *The Little Book of Yoga Breathing: Pranayama Made Easy.* Red Wheel/Weiser, 2005.

Shipman, Sara. *Real Life Astrology: The Planets in Signs*. Published by the author, 2021.

Shipman, Sara. *Real Life Astrology: Planets, Signs & Houses*. Published by the author, 2024.

Solomon, Kathilyn. *Tapping Into Wellness: Using EFT to Clear Emotional & Physical Pain & Illness*. Llewellyn Publications, 2015.

Swann, Eliza. *Auras: The Anatomy of the Aura (A Start Here Guide for Beginners)*. St. Martin's Essentials, 2020.

Todeschi, Kevin J., and Carol Ann Liaros. *Edgar Cayce on Auras & Colors: Learn to Understand Color and See Auras*. A.R.E Press, 2012.

Usui, Mikao, and Frank Arjava Petter. *The Original Reiki Handbook of Dr. Mikao Usui: The Traditional Usui Reiki Ryoho Treatment Positions and Numerous Reiki Techniques for Health and Well-Being.* Lotus Press, 1999.

Watkins, Alfred. *The Old Straight Track: Its Mounds, Beacons, Moats, Sites and Mark Stones*. Heritage Hunter, 2016.

Wild, Elsie. *The Little Book of Chakras: An Introduction to Ancient Wisdom and Spiritual Healing.* Summersdale, 2021.

Wildwood, Rob. *Magical Britain: 650 Enchanted and Mystical Sites — From Healing Wells and Secret Shrines to Giants' Strongholds and Fairy Glens*. Wild Things Publishing, 2022.

Bibliography

Agrippa, Heinrich Cornelius. *Three Books of Occult Philosophy by Heinrich Cornelius Agrippa.* Translated by James Freake. Lost Book Project, 2024, Kindle.

Aromatherapy Trade Council. "How to Use Essential Oils." Accessed March 31, 2025. https://www.a-t-c.org.uk/about-aromatherapy/how-to-use-essential-oils/.

Britannica. "Nymphaeum." Accessed March 31, 2025. https://www.britannica.com/art/nymphaeum.

Guarneri, Erminia, and Rauni Prittinen King. "Challenges and Opportunities Faced by Biofield Practitioners in Global Health and Medicine: A White Paper." Supplement. *Global Advances in Health and Medicine* 4. No. SI (2015). https://pmc.ncbi.nlm.nih.gov/articles/PMC4654785/.

Hofer, Andrew, and Jonah Teller. *Nine Days with Saint Michael.* Magnificat, 2021. Kindle.

International Federation of Aromatherapists. "Legislation Affecting Aromatherapists and Product Designers." Accessed March 31, 2025. https://ifaroma.org/en_GB/home/registrants/aromatherapy-legislation.

Michell, John. *The View over Atlantis.* Abacus, 1973.

National Center for Complementary and Alternative Medicine. "NCCIH Timeline." Accessed March 31, 2025. https://www.nccih.nih.gov/about/nccih-timeline.

Nelson, Bradley. *The Emotion Code: How to Release Your Trapped Emotions for Abundant Health, Love, and Happiness*. Vermillion, 2019.

The Old Operating Theatre Museum and Herb Garret. "About Us." Accessed March 31, 2025. https://oldoperatingtheatre.com/about-us/.

Simon Fraser University Public Knowledge Project Archives. Accessed March 31, 2025. https://journals.sfu.ca/seemj/index.php/seemj/issue/archive.

Todeschi, Kevin J., and Carol Ann Liaros. *Edgar Cayce on Auras & Colors: Learn to Understand Color and See Auras.* A.R.E Press, 2012. Kindle.

Usui, Mikao, and Frank Arjava Petter. *The Original Reiki Handbook of Dr. Mikao Usui: The Traditional Usui Reiki Ryoho Treatment Positions and Numerous Reiki Techniques for Health and Well-Being.* Lotus Press, 1999. Kindle.

Watkins, Alfred. *The Old Straight Track: Its Mounds, Beacons, Moats, Sites and Mark Stones*. Heritage Hunter, 2016. Kindle.

Index

A

Acupuncture, 6, 72
Akashic records, 65
Amulets, 11
Angelic healing, 117, 119, 205
Angelic Reiki, 119
Angels, 53, 87, 117–120, 126, 129, 149, 154, 178, 205
Astral travel, 19
Auras, 2, 3, 61, 65, 88, 104–112, 121, 177

B

Bagua map, 183–186
Binaural beats, 136, 137
Body scan, 63, 112, 162, 169, 171, 177
Breathwork, 26, 34, 39, 47

C

Centring, 3, 26, 29–33, 36, 42, 47, 63, 70, 79, 81, 89, 93, 94, 101, 125, 127, 149, 173, 197, 203
Chakras, 1–3, 5, 32, 39, 51, 53, 61, 63, 65, 85–106, 108, 112–116, 119–121, 123, 135, 136, 165, 166, 169, 170, 174, 178, 208
Charms, 11, 51, 154, 169, 185, 198
Chi, 6
Cleansing, 1–3, 8, 9, 11, 19, 20, 30, 45, 54–59, 62, 66, 67, 88–90, 92, 93, 96, 97, 101, 102, 114, 115, 129, 132, 143, 150, 162, 163, 165, 167, 171, 173–177, 180, 182, 193, 195–197, 202, 206, 207

Collective consciousness, 64, 65
Colour healing, 3, 39, 61, 64, 68
Consent, 14, 160
Crown chakra, 53, 98, 99, 102, 103, 106, 108, 116, 136
Crystal grids, 120–123, 126, 128, 129, 166, 178, 183, 197, 204
Crystal healing, 2, 78, 120, 136, 160, 178, 197
Crystals, 2, 16, 22, 26, 39–43, 52–56, 61, 72, 86, 88, 90, 92–94, 96, 97, 99, 117, 119–123, 128–130, 138, 140, 142–149, 152, 155, 160, 163–167, 169, 171, 173, 176, 178, 191, 197, 204, 208

D

Divination, 96, 131, 165, 177
Divine Gateway chakra, 87
Dowsing rods, 164, 202
Dream interpretation, 1, 72, 141, 166, 181, 191

E

Earth Star chakra, 87
Egg cleanse, 56, 57
Emotion Code, 60
Emotional freedom technique (EFT), 3, 63, 72, 74, 78–84, 112, 113, 117, 160, 178
Energy, 1–22, 24–27, 30–34, 36–43, 45–51, 53–68, 70, 72–74, 78, 85–91, 93–106, 108–117, 119, 120, 123–155, 157, 159–167, 170, 171, 173–179, 181–183, 186, 187, 189, 190, 193–195, 198, 202–208
Energy attacks, 15, 18, 19, 49
Energy blockages, 63, 64, 73, 86, 90, 93, 95, 104, 110–113, 132–136, 144–148, 162, 164, 165, 177–179
Energy orbs, 26, 37–39, 43, 47, 63, 101, 115, 167, 204
Energy scanning, 20, 100
Energy vampirism, 16, 18
Essential oils, 51, 55, 152, 193, 196, 197
Ethics, 2, 3, 5, 14, 17, 24, 49, 59, 161

F
Feng shui, 182–188, 191, 193, 194, 206

G
Galactic chakra, 87
Gratitude journal, 14
Grounding, 3, 26, 29–31, 42, 72, 89, 114, 121, 136, 163, 169
Guides, 8, 22, 24, 52, 87, 97, 159

H
Hag stones, 198
Hara, 32
Heart chakra, 93–95, 103, 105, 136, 166

I
Incantation, 52
Irish ogham, 131, 133, 134

J
Jupiter, 51, 138, 139, 146, 147

K
Karmic consequences, 15, 24

L
Ley lines, 164, 198–203, 206
Lithomancy, 165

M
Magic square, 51, 138–140, 152, 205
Mantras, 14, 64, 83, 89, 91, 92, 94, 96, 98, 99, 152, 170
Mars, 138, 144, 145
Meditation, 2, 5, 22, 26–31, 33, 38, 39, 47, 49, 52, 62, 63, 67, 73, 89, 98, 99, 101–103, 111, 112, 137, 142, 151, 157–159, 163, 173, 190, 204, 205, 207

Mercury, 138, 143, 144
Meridians, 6, 61, 68–73, 78–82, 85, 169
Monitoring, 174, 177, 178, 180
Moon, 8, 67, 134, 137–143, 150, 151

N

National Center for Complementary and Alternative Medicine (NCCAM), 7
Nature spirits, 117, 153, 158, 159
Negative energy, 4, 5, 8–11, 15, 16, 18–20, 24, 27, 46, 48–50, 54, 55, 58, 102, 103, 165, 166, 174–176, 181
Negative energy attachments, 20
Neptune, 138, 148, 152

O

Oracle cards, 165

P

Pendulums, 164, 165, 177, 202
Planets, 51, 65, 137–141, 143–146, 148–153, 205
Pluto, 138, 149
Poppets, 160, 162, 167–171
Power centre, 3, 26, 32, 33, 42, 47, 63, 101, 173
Power crystal, 166
Prana, 5, 7, 8, 34, 117
Pranayama, 36
Protection, 1–3, 11, 18, 45, 46, 50–53, 58, 62, 118, 121, 126, 130, 133, 154, 162, 169, 174, 176, 177, 180, 182, 197, 198, 207
Psychometry, 40
Putative energy, 8

Q

Qi, 6, 8, 73, 74, 117, 182, 186–189, 193, 194
Qi Gong, 6, 8, 61, 73, 74, 98, 163, 173, 177

R

Reflexology, 6, 8
Reiki, 8, 16, 23, 32, 33, 38, 63, 98, 99, 110, 112–117, 119, 120, 135, 160, 170, 178, 205
Ritual bath, 54, 55
Rituals, 1, 52, 54, 55, 62, 68, 156, 174, 175
Root chakra, 86–90, 102, 103, 105, 136, 169

S

Sachets, 52, 53, 176
Sacral chakra, 85, 86, 89–91, 103, 105, 136, 166
Sacred geometry, 120–122, 124, 166
Saturn, 138, 147, 151
Scrying, 96, 166
Shielding, 18, 39–40, 46–50, 68, 112, 173
Showering, 9, 45, 55, 165, 173, 175, 178, 180
Smoke cleanse, 54, 56, 165, 171, 173, 175, 196
Society for the Study of Subtle Energies and Energy Medicine, 6
Solar plexus chakra, 32, 39, 86, 91–93, 95, 105, 136, 165
Solar Star chakra, 87
Solfeggio frequencies, 136
Soul Star chakra, 87
Sound bath, 54, 56, 135, 173, 175, 178
Sound healing, 2, 7, 13, 24, 29, 56, 61, 64, 72, 86, 89, 93, 98, 110, 130, 135, 136, 165, 178, 179, 195
Strengthening energy, 27, 49, 50, 88, 101, 102, 110, 173, 174, 179, 180
Sun, 8, 67, 129, 137, 138, 142–144, 150, 189, 194
Symbols, 50–54, 65, 106, 107, 112–115, 118, 120, 122–124, 131, 138–140, 142–149, 152, 158, 176, 178, 205, 207

T

Tai chi, 6
Tarot cards, 22, 165, 166

Third eye chakra, 51, 96–98, 102, 103, 105, 136
Throat chakra, 86, 94–96, 103, 105, 136
Tree energy, 61, 130, 131, 178

U

Universal energy, 2, 6–8, 18, 31, 34, 46, 47, 55, 63, 73, 98, 99, 102, 112–115, 117, 119, 124, 127, 133, 136, 160, 163, 167, 207
Uranus, 138, 148, 149
Usui Reiki, 32, 33, 110, 113

V

Veiling, 53
Venus, 138, 144–146, 149, 151
Veritable energy, 7

W

White light visualisation, 31, 34, 55, 102, 115, 119–120, 175

Y

Yoga, 5, 90, 98

To Write to the Author

If you wish to contact the author or would like more information about this book, please write to the author in care of Llewellyn Worldwide Ltd. and we will forward your request. Both the author and the publisher appreciate hearing from you and learning of your enjoyment of this book and how it has helped you. Llewellyn Worldwide Ltd. cannot guarantee that every letter written to the author can be answered, but all will be forwarded. Please write to:

Jessica Howard
℅ Llewellyn Worldwide
2143 Wooddale Drive
Woodbury, MN 55125-2989

Please enclose a self-addressed stamped envelope for reply, or $1.00 to cover costs. If outside the U.S.A., enclose an international postal reply coupon.

Many of Llewellyn's authors have websites with additional information and resources. For more information, please visit our website at https://www.llewellyn.com.